391 BEA

Beard, Tyler
100 years of Western wear

NORFOLK PUBLIC LIBRARY
308 PROSPECT AVENUE
NORFOLK, NE 68701
THERE IS NO GRACE PERIOD
ON THIS BOOK. BOOK IS
DUE ON LAST DATE STAMPED.

100 Years of Western Wear

NORFOLK PUBLIC LIBRARY
NORFOLK, NEBRASKA

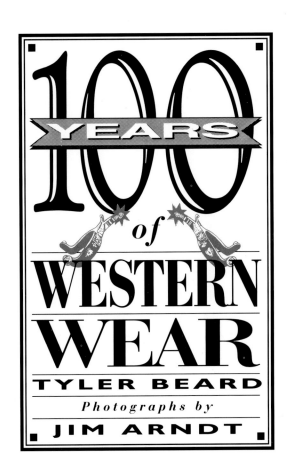

100 YEARS of WESTERN WEAR

TYLER BEARD

Photographs by

JIM ARNDT

GIBBS·SMITH PUBLISHER

SALT LAKE CITY

To my grandparents:
  Claud, Jimmie Lee,
  Clara, and Guy.

First edition
98 97 96 95 94 93   10 9 8 7 6 5 4 3 2 1

Text copyright © 1993 by Tyler Beard
Photographs copyright © 1993 by Jim Arndt, unless otherwise noted

All rights reserved. No part of this book may be reproduced by any
means whatsoever, either electronic or mechanical, without written
permission from the publisher, except for brief excerpts quoted for the
purpose of review.

This is a Peregrine Smith Book, published by
Gibbs Smith, Publisher
P.O. Box 667
Layton, Utah 84041

Design by J. Scott Knudsen, Park City, Utah
Front cover photograph © 1993 by Jim Arndt, from Tyler and Teresa
  Beard collection, concha belt from Jim Arndt collection.
Back cover photographs by Jim Arndt.

Library of Congress Cataloging-in-Publication Data
Beard, Tyler, 1954-
One hundred years of Western wear / Tyler Beard ; Jim Arndt,
photographer.
p. cm.
ISBN 0-87905-581-2
ISBN 0-87905-591-X (pbk.)
1. Costume—West (U.S.)—History. I. Arndt, Jim. II. Title. III. Title:
100 years of Western wear.
GT617.W47B43 1993
391'.00978—dc20   93-14072
                                         CIP
Printed in Hong Kong

A howdy and a thanks go out to all the folks whose interest, knowledge, enthusiasm, and love for western wear and all things western helped make this book possible. I am grateful to the following:

Jim Arndt for his never-ending enthusiasm and photographic talent.

Craig and Niles (of Egypt) for all the fun, wake-up calls, and "stylin'."

Madge Baird, my Utah friend, who does the work of four.

Gary van der Meer, my NYC "boot twin," who always goes beyond the call of duty.

Don and Vicki Smith for their red-carpet treatment and Oklahoma hospitality.

Byron Price and Richard Rattenbury, The National Cowboy Hall of Fame Museum, Oklahoma City, Oklahoma.

Manuel (the one and only), Nashville, Tennessee.

Norma Paz (at Manuel's).

Chris Skinker, curator of collections, Country Music Foundation, Nashville, Tennessee.

Margaret Formby, executive director and president, and Virginia Autho, assistant director, The Cowgirl Hall of Fame Museum, Hereford, Texas.

Roy Rogers.

Dusty Rogers, Roy Rogers and Dale Evans Museum, Victorville, California.

Gene and Jackie Autry.

The folks at The Gene Autry Western Heritage Museum, Los Angeles, California: James Nottage, chief curator; Jim Wilke; Susan Deland; and Joanne Hale, chief executive officer and director.

Kathy Barrett for the whirlwind California tour.

He may be "Little" Jimmy Dickens, but he is big on heart and soul.

Bo and Pam Riddle, Nashville, Tennessee.

Nathalie Kent and Jill (our redneck girl).

Rusty Summerville, design manager, Grand Ole Opry Museum at Opryland USA, Nashville, Tennessee.

Brenda Haas, registrar at Panhandle-Plains Historical Museum, Canyon, Texas.

Charlie Seeman.

Rose Maddox.

Linda Hand at Wrangler.

Hank Thompson.

Rodeo Ben, Jr. (I could listen to those stories for a month).

Tootsies, for cold refreshments and a good Webb Pierce imitator.

Bill and Betty, aka "Stormy Jo," for slipping me into denim, fringe, boots, embroidered shirts, hats, and holsters at age four. "Western wear will never die."

And finally, my lovely wife, my "Queen of the West," who never thought I would finish this book either.

TYLER BEARD

I would like to thank the following people for all their help on this book:

First, my crew at the studio: Kelly Jo Johnson, Curtis Johnson, Steve Goodwin, Nils Rahm, and Mark Palas.

Thanks to all the people along the road who helped make this book happen: our publisher, Gibbs Smith, and our editor, Madge Baird; Manuel and Norma; Nathalie Kent; Dusty Rogers; Gary van der Meer of Billy Martins; Spencer and Jack Pressler; Wendy Lane; Jane Smith and her wonderful staff; all of the very professional help at the many museums; and of course, Gene Autry and Roy Rogers.

And special thanks to Tyler Beard for all his help, patience, and enthusiasm which kept this project going, and to his wife, Teresa, for letting Tyler go on the road again and for putting up with us. A special thanks also to Connie Evingson for all her support and understanding.

And last, a very large "thank you" to Craig Gjerness for all his help in keeping this project together and helping me shoot the photographs for this book.

JIM ARNDT

Introduction   11

1890–1930
Cowboy and Cowgirl Style: The Beginnings   16

1930–1970
Nashville Meets Hollywood: The Golden Years of Western Wear   30

1970–1990
The Fall of Western Wear: Hippies, Polyester, Western Grunge,
Urban Cowboys, and Redneck Chic   112

1890-1990
Gallery of Western Wear   116

The 1990s
Western Couture Goes Wild: One Hundred Years of
Influence Come Together   125

Source Guide   151

(Photo National Cowboy Hall of Fame)

WHERE THE WEST BEGINS

Out where the handclasp's a little stronger,
Out where the smile dwells a little longer,
    That's where the West begins;
Out where the sun is a little brighter,
Where the snows that fall are a trifle whiter;
Where the bonds of home are a wee bit tighter;
    That's where the West begins;
Out where the skies are a trifle bluer,
Out where the friendship's a little truer,
    That's where the West begins;
Out where a fresher breeze is blowing,
Where there's laughter in every streamlet flowing,
Where there's more of reaping and less of sowing,
    That's where the West begins;
Out where the world is in the making,
Where fewer hearts with despair are aching;
    That's where the West begins;
Where there's more of singing and less of sighing,
Where there's more of giving and less of buying,
And a man makes friends without half trying,
    That's where the West begins.

—*ARTHUR CHAPMAN*

*T*he Flamboyant Fraternity, *left to right: Elisha Green, Wild Bill Hickok, Buffalo Bill Cody, Texas Jack Omohundro, and Eugene Overton. This photo, taken in 1873, indicates that the mountain men, buffalo hunters, trappers, and early frontiersmen were idolized by these men the same way we emulate cowboys from later decades. It is interesting to see that in the 1990s, clothing with twisted fringe, beaded leather, and embroidery are all experiencing a revival for men's and women's western wear—more than a hundred years after this photograph was taken. (Photo Buffalo Bill Historical Center)*

To unravel the origins of western wear, we would have to go back thousands of years to any civilization known for its horsemen. Let us begin in 1769, when Franciscan missionaries brought in small herds of longhorn cattle from Mexico to Spanish California and the Lower Rio Grande Valley in what was to become Texas.

On the *rancheros*, these men developed the basic ranching techniques, cowboy vocabulary, and the earliest western style that is still recognizable in all cowboys today. The North American cowboy appeared a full half century after those missionary cowboys, or *vaqueros*.

Some of the Spanish terms that hang on in cowboying today are:

Vaco, or *vaquero*, meaning cow.

La riata became lariat.

Chaparreras was shortened to chaps.

Dar la vuelta translates to "make a turn," what the North American cowboy calls dallying the rope around the saddle horn.

The tall-crowned sombrero was the model for the cowboy hat, and as with most vaquero legacy, the spurs came to them from Spain.

Richard Dana wrote about the vaquero in 1840:

His broad brimmed hat usually of a black or dark brown color, with a gilt or figured band around the crown, and lined under the rim with silk; a short jacket of silk or figured calico . . . the

shirt open in the back; rich waistcoat, if any; pantaloons open at the sides below the knee, laced with gilt, usually of velveteen or brown cloth; or else short breeches or white stockings . . . they have no suspenders, but always wear a sash around the waist, which is generally red, and varying in quality with the means of the wearer. Add to this the never-failing poncho or serape, and you have the dress of the Californian.

The poor early Texas cowboy's clothing was anything but decorative. The basic design elements were developed for protection, much like the armor of a knight. The North American cowboy continued to redefine his image throughout the 1870s, which prompted old-time Texas cowboy Will S. James to write:

During the war his clothing was made from home-spun cloth, he had no other, home-made shoes or boots, even his hat was home-made—, the favorite hat material being straw. Rye straw was the best. Sometimes a fellow would get hold of a Mexican hat, and then he was sailing. . . . By 1972 most everything on the ranch had undergone a change. . . . But especially had style changed, the wool hat, the leather leggins. . . . The style changed again by '77. The John B. Stetson hat with a deeper crown and not too broad a rim, and the ten-ounce hat took the cake. Up to this date, the

In the 1890s—before rodeo cowgirls, dude ranches, and Hollywood westerns—
there were precious few rough-and-tumble women in the West. Calamity Jane
held the reins. For the most part, the women who traveled west came with their
families. Their clothing was standard Victorian, with high collars, button
sleeves, long skirts, straw hats, and eyelet boots. This photograph of the Becker
sisters branding cattle on their father's ranch was taken in 1894. Divided
skirts were worn in the 1890s in some areas of the West. They were a practical
solution to comfortable horseback riding and ranch work. Out of necessity,
ranch women slowly began to wear standard dry-good clothes which were
similar in style and durability to what their brothers and husbands wore.
(Photo Colorado Historical Society)

high-heeled boots were the rage, and
when it was possible to have them, the
heel was made to start under the foot,
for what reason I never knew, unless it
was the same motive that prompts the
gals to wear the opera heel in order to
make a small track, thus leaving the
impression that number ten was only a
six.

By the late 1870s, the cattle industry was
booming in Texas, and the emerging North

American cowboy, as we know him, had
developed his own style of dressing, borrow-
ing only the basic origins of his appearance
from his vaquero predecessors.

This book is an overview of the basic history of western wear, focusing on the golden
era, 1930–70. Without excluding other
decades entirely, we have supplied a brief
look at our earliest western-wear origins
through the nineteenth-century cowboy.

Buried somewhere deep in the soul,
every American is just a little bit cowboy or
cowgirl achin' to get out. Part sex symbol,
part hero, part myth, for more than a century
these brave idols of the West have continued
to touch people's lives all over the world.
The cowboy is larger than life and continues
to be a part of our cultural consciousness in
the 1990s.

The West is not a place. The West is a
state of mind.

*R*eal working cowboys in typical turn-of-the-century gear.
(Photo National Cowboy Hall of Fame)

*T*he Belle of the Ranch *is obviously not really a cowgirl or ranch woman. This highly romanticized studio shot was taken in 1909. (Photo courtesy Tyler Beard)*

*G*aston Boykin, now 87, was a working cowboy for
12 years. In 1926, when this photograph was
taken, he had just driven 47 wild horses from Ozona,
Texas, to Comanche, Texas with three other cowboys.
Gaston was sheriff in Comanche County between
1947 and 1977. (Photo courtesy Gaston Boykin)

*A*lthough western wear was well on its way in the 1920s, common sportswear was still part of the western look. In this photo, there are no trophy buckles or ranger sets, only small rectangular initial buckles—worn by most of the men in the early 1900s, cowboy or not. The oversized hat and bandana were obviously required parts of the costume. The waist sash is a vaquero influence which, by 1930, had almost disappeared from fashion. (Photo courtesy Pro Rodeo Hall of Fame and Museum of the American Cowboy)

*J*ackson Sundown, who claimed to be the nephew of Chief Joseph, was the first and only full-blooded Indian to ever win a major rodeo championship: at the Pendleton Roundup in 1916, at age 53, he won the saddle bronc riding event. When asked what inscription he wanted on the trophy, he replied, "Please put wife's name." Sundown, with Indian-style braids, was proud of his heritage and wore beaded fringed gauntlets, had feathers in his hat, and wore colorful silk ribbons to hold his hat down tight. On occasion, he would dress in complete traditional Nez Perce costume. Throughout his short and colorful rodeo career, these orange Angora chaps with black spots remained this buckaroo's trademark. (Photo from Matt Johnson, Howdyshell Collection, Pendleton, Oregon)

1890–1930
COWBOY AND COWGIRL STYLE: THE BEGINNING

In the 1890s, the cowboy, from whom all of our basic western wear's origins sprang, had a uniform that varied from man to man based on his desire to be an individual and have his own style. The other factors of his appearance were where he lived and what particular job he performed. Let's start at the top:

The average cowboy wore a Stetson hat called a JB, which stood for John B. Stetson. The "Boss" was the first model; the "Carlsbad" was the most popular in the Stetson line. And if you wanted a higher and wider hat, there were always the "Buckeye" and the "Montana Peak." Durability was the virtue of the Stetson hat. You could soak it, dirty it, stomp on it, or shoot a hole clean through it, and with little effort it would retain its original character and shape. The imitators all came later.

The ever-present bandana was usually red or blue and served as a multipurpose

I have affectionately named this cowgirl "Squirrel Girl" because of the pelt sewn to her skirt. This photo was taken about 1910. You can tell that Annie Oakley and Calamity Jane were influential among the female followers of fashion, even in their own day. (Photo courtesy Tyler Beard)

tool out West. A cowboy always wore long sleeves with a three-to-five-button placket in the front to keep the cold out in the winter. His shirt was usually hickory or linsey-woolsey, especially in the wintertime. In the summertime, pinstripe, collarless, Victorian-style shirts were preferred.

In all seasons and in all regions, almost every cowboy wore a vest, usually a standard dry-good garment of wool or corduroy, in shades of gray, blue, brown, or black. The vest was essential, for it had pockets to hold makin's for a cigarette, a pocket watch, or perhaps a pencil and a book for marking brands and counting cattle.

California pants were made of heavy, rugged wool in striped or checkered designs. Contrary to popular belief, most cowboys preferred these to Levis in the 1890s. In warmer weather, a cowboy wore trousers made of cotton nankeen—a tough, durable cotton imported from China. Commonly,

*T*he hat (worn by Walter Brennan in westerns such as Red River *with* John Wayne), woollies, rawhide rope, single-row stitched boots, spurs and leathers with a single concha all recreate the mood of the 1890s. In reality, these items were similar from the 1880s through the 1920s. As with all clothing and artifacts, it is sometimes difficult to determine exactly what year they were made. (Courtesy National Cowboy Hall of Fame)

Pre-1924 cowgirls, left to right: Kitty Canutt, Prairie Rose, and Ruth Roach in typical cowgirl garb of the time—oversized hats; lace, silk, and oriental embroidered blouses; suede skirts and riding bloomers; tall-top high-heeled boots; and spurs. (Photo National Cowgirl Hall of Fame Museum)

these trousers were reinforced with leather in the seat and legs for riding.

As time went on, cowboys began to accept the cool comfort and easy care of Levis, an inexpensive cowboy work pant. Galusses, better known as suspenders, held up their pants; otherwise, they wore tight waists. Most work pants, including Levis, had a belt in the back that could be cinched in to tighten the waist. Belt loops did not appear on Levis until 1922.

Gloves and gauntlets were made of deerskin, horsehide, elk, or goatskin to protect the wearer's hands from rope burns and the cold. In northern regions, heavy mittens made from buffalo, bear, wolf, and other fur-bearing critters were a must for winter. The hand was leather and the lining usually wide-welt corduroy or wool. Many cowboys wore leather wrist cuffs, whose popularity peaked in the 1930s.

Chaps were worn by almost every working cowboy. These were seatless coverings that protected against ropes, brush, horse bite, and inclement weather. In the 1890s, shotgun chaps were the common style. These had straight legs with or without side fringe. Bat-wings (also called Texas legs) were loose in the leg and wider in the front, making them easier to get in and out of. Last but not least were the woollies—step-in chaps with sheepskin or Angora goat-hide fronts which made them warm in the winter. Other snappy chappies were covered in mountain lion, pony skin, bear, and buffalo.

Boots in the 1890s drew heavily on cavalry and Civil War styles. What is referred to as the first cowboy-boot style was made of softer leather with decorative stitching which assisted in keeping the boots upright. These boots had inside canvas cloth pull straps, leather inside straps, or long mule ears which hung down the outside of the boot and made tugging the boots on a might easier. The toes were either square or round and generally two to three inches wide.

Spurs varied in design more than anything else the cowboy wore. The spur shank, buttons, and rowel came in an assortment of shapes and styles. The cowboy longed for music out on the lone prairie, and with his jingle bobs, janglers, and boot chains, he was a one-man minstrel show. He could hear himself coming a mile away, and so could everybody else. Spur leathers also ranged from plain-Jane to fancy. Some of them were tooled in floral designs and maybe even had a leather or silver concha for decoration on the side.

A cowboy wore either a tough leather or canvas ducking brush jacket, or Mackinaw-style blanket coat in plain or checkered wool. In the dust he wore a lightweight, light-colored, full-length coverall-type coat with large pockets and a split up the back to accommo-

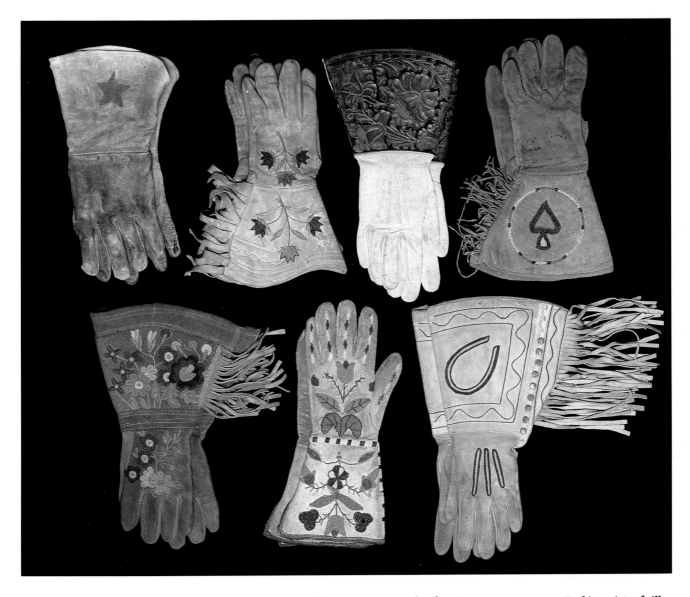

GAUNTLETS

Gloves extending above the wrist for extra protection, gauntlets were worn by men and women for everyday work, rodeos, and Wild West shows. The fringed gauntlet, plain and decorated, is experiencing a revival in the 1990s—and not just on the urban cowboys and cowgirls. I recently helped eight real working cowpokes round up, brand, dehorn, castrate and vaccinate 200 head of cattle, and by gosh, two of them were wearin' fringed gauntlets.

date his saddle—this was called a duster. In the wet, he would unroll from behind his saddle his slicker, or "Fish" (a brand name that became synonymous with raincoat or slicker from the 1870s to 1950s).

Most women on the frontier wore a sunbonnet; a calico dress with a high collar and long sleeves; and kid, cloth, or leather button-up boots. For weddings, funerals, or just goin' to town, the Victorian influence was still prevalent in women's clothing well into the twentieth century. However, by 1910, Annie Oakley, Calamity Jane, and other Wild West stars—such as Edith Tantlinger, leading cowgirl of the Miller 101 Wild West Show; May Lillie, star and wife of Pawnee Bill; Annie Scafer, the first lady bronc rider; Lucille Mulhall, who was called the first "real" rodeo cowgirl—and dozens of others paved the way for future cowgirls.

In 1914 Philip Ashton Rollins wrote about the woman's role on a western ranch:

This variety of silk-embroidered, beaded, spotted, fringed and tooled leather gauntlets range in date from 1870 to 1930. (National Cowboy Hall of Fame)

***B**rain-tanned buckskin jacket with sinew seams, delicate floral beadwork, and railroad-conductor brass buttons from Canada is Indian-made. (Brain tanning is a process where the brains of the animal are applied to the skin for additional softening.) The buttons were probably acquired in a barter. This beaded and fringed jacket shows how early mountain men's style—which is considered to be the first form of western wear—borrowed heavily from the Indians. (Tyler and Teresa Beard collection)*

There were, it is true, permanently living on a number of ranches women. . . . The horse being the principal and often only means of transit, many of these women and many of their daughters rode extremely well. The side-saddles and woolen riding-skirts used by most of these women, the modest divided skirts used by the few who rode astride, imparted to those quiet, unassuming courageous females of the real frontier none of the garishness which that modern invention, the buckskin-clad "cowgirl," takes with her into the circus ring.

These "cowgirls" may be of Western spirit and blood, but their buckskin clothing speaks of the present-day theatre and not the ranches of long ago.

New styles are never without some social censure. The slow acceptance of the changes in early western wear for women shines through in this excerpt from a ranch woman's diary:

First I discarded, or rather refused to adopt, the sunbonnet, conventional headgear of my female neighbors. When I went unashamedly about under a five-gallon Stetson, many an eyebrow was raised; then followed a double-breasted blue flannel shirt with white pearl buttons, frankly unfeminine. In time came blue denim nickers worn under a short blue denim skirt. Slow evolution (or was it decadence?) toward a costume suited for immediate needs. Decadence having set in, the descent from the existing standards of female modesty to purely human comfort and convenience was swift. A man's saddle and a divided riding skirt was inevitable. This was the nineties.

By the end of the 1890s, cowboys and Wild West showmen were well aware that their mystique had traveled east and west around the world. Tall tales in dime novels, pulps, and newspaper serials kept the cowboy aware of what he should look like. The early movie *The Great Train Robbery* was followed by William S. Hart's films, in which Hart insisted on authenticity in all of the clothing. Silent movies and talkies included real working cowboys and reservation Indians as extras. Hart focused on the rough and tough cowboy, the rugged individual

MONTANA FRANK SHOWS

who was self-reliant, honest, fearless, and independent. Into the 1920s, Hart was followed by Ken Maynard, Bob Steele, Harry Carey, Buck Jones, Hoot Gibson, Jack Hoxie, and Tim McCoy. All of these screen cowboys had an immense impact on what we call today "classic western wear." Western movies since 1911 have relied on Western Costume Company of Los Angeles to outfit casts with realistic western clothing from all eras.

More than any other star before 1930, Tom Mix had the greatest influence on western wear as an emerging style for the masses. Tom Mix was a sexy sight, with his good looks, E. H. Bohlin gear, flashy boots with high heels and solid silver jeweled spurs, sweeping "Montana Peak" Stetson hat, and silk and satin corded and embroidered shirts with western yokes and bib fronts. Mix was equivalent to a rock star of today.

The first Wild West shows began with Buffalo Bill in 1882. The forerunners of our modern rodeo, they were a combination circus, historical drama, and rodeo. Their popularity continued into the 1930s until the depression, when the cost and logistics of traveling to various cities became prohibitive. Holster, belt, and Colt dated 1909, spotted cuffs 1920s, spotted quirt made from fancy reins 1920s, Chihuahua spurs about 1900, beaded and fringed jacket 1930s. (Tyler and Teresa Beard Collection)

On October 12, 1940, the newspapers reported that Tom Mix was killed en route to Phoenix, Arizona, when he swerved to miss a road crew in his custom-built Cord roadster with longhorns mounted on the radiator. Tom was wearing his trademark ten-gallon white Stetson hat, cream-colored cowboy suit with western-trimmed yokes and scarlet whipcord, and black patent-leather boots with a floral design stitched in red, white, and blue silk thread. He wore a diamond-studded platinum belt buckle with the famous TM brand, which was on everything he owned—right down to his underwear.

These intricately decorated and conchaed bat-wing chaps were made by R. T. Frazier in 1913 and sold through his mail-order catalog for $42. The current owner has turned down offers as high as $6,000. (Joe Gish collection)

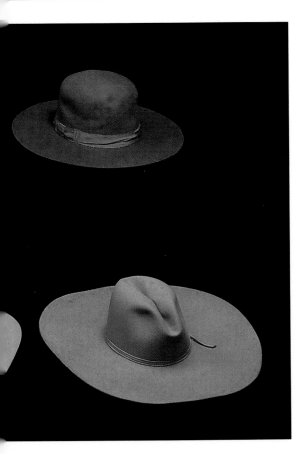

Top row, left to right: Texas pattern by Rekcud, 1880–85; southwestern peak by Stetson, 1910–15; custom crease by Stetson worn by Will James, 1920–25; and ten-gallon rodeo pattern Stetson worn by Tad Lucas, 1930–35. Bottom row, left to right: oversized rodeo and show pattern custom-made by Resistol for Fay Kirkwood, 1940–45; box crease Stetson, 1950–55; contemporary style by Eddy Brothers, 1965–75; urban cowboy and country-music pattern by Charlie 1 Horse, 1980–85; and contemporary dress pattern by Resistol, 1989–90. (Courtesy National Cowboy Hall of Fame)

HATS

The hat has always been a crown of individualism. Originally, western hats were available only in a few shades of taupe and tan. Black followed, then white, then every color in the crayon box. Popular hat creases change every so often, due to the popularity of a certain celebrity's style; yet all hats considered, there has been little change overall in the cowboy hat. A certain crease and hatband can create a personal touch.

For the first fifty years, all hats came with a dome or open crown, and the buyer had to choose a crease at the hat shop or do it at home. If you study old group photos taken at rodeos or roundups, almost all the hats are different. It was a point of pride, so much that a man could be recognized in silhouette only, by his hat crease, which prompted some ranch churches to cut out hat racks in their entryways in the shape of the members' various hat styles.

On the back of this photograph in faded pencil, you can just make out "Sandy Oakley, 1916." I wonder if she's related.... (Photo courtesy Tyler Beard)

*F*rom 1900 until the early 1930s, most rodeo cowgirl couture was made at
home or on the road. These navy-blue wool trousers with white appliqued
arrows and stripes were the peg-legged bloomer of jodhpur style worn in the
early 1900s–20s. Shoes or boots were topped off with fancy silver-button
leggings. These pants belonged to rodeo cowgirl Juanita Howell, whose famous
rodeo mother was The Prairie Fawn. The leggings were worn by Reine Shelton,
who stunned audiences with her stunts on horseback with Buffalo Bill, Colonel
Gordon Lilly, and the 101 Wild West Show. (National Cowgirl Hall of Fame
collection)

These tall boots with spurs, pre-1900, are the earliest cowgirl boots known. The other pair, pre-1930, are stitched with a longhorn pattern and have period spurs. (Jim Holley collection)

A collection of authentic cowboy bandanas dating from 1870 to 1920. (Tyler and Teresa Beard collection)

BANDANA

Call it what you will—bandana, neckerchief, scarf, wild rag, or muffler—it was the cowboy's best friend. Cowboys preferred red or blue bandanas and simple calicoes, flower motifs, polka dots and paisleys. The bandana helped the cowboy ward off dust, wash his face, tie up broken bones, and signal his friends, and it even helped some outlaws rob trains and banks.

Martha Washington is credited with creating the first American bandana in 1775. It was a patriotic souvenir, intended to boost morale during the Revolution. In the 1890s, Buffalo Bill's Wild West shows sold souvenir bandanas with Buffalo Bill's and Sitting Bull's likenesses printed on the fabric.

Teddy Roosevelt, the cowboy president, handed out red cowboy neckerchiefs emblazoned with a caricature of himself and little TRs around the borders during both of his presidential campaigns.

It was not until the 1920s that rodeo promoters began to market "wild rags"—silk and satin scarves decorated with western scenes, broncs, and slogans.

Hyer Boot Company of Olathe, Kansas, made this lace-up shoe boot in the "packer" style for rodeo contestant Frank Finch in 1926. Packers were popular from the late 1800s to the 1930s, then were almost unseen until the 1980s, when custom boot makers began producing them for working cowboys in the Northwest. Justin Boot Company now has its own popular version called the Lace-up Roper for women and men. (National Cowboy Hall of Fame)

Vera McGinnis was the cowgirl who rode the fastest and dared the most. She performed in more foreign countries than any other cowgirl of her time. Vera was the first woman to wear long pants in place of the split riding skirt in the rodeo, around 1924. (Photo National Cowgirl Hall of Fame Museum)

String ties and silk bandanas, called "Let 'Er Buck" scarves or cowboy mufflers in the catalogs, were popular from the 1920s through the 1940s. These bandanas are gathered with western-motif bolo slides. The bandanas came in dozens of colors and designs and cost 75–95¢. After World War II, the designs were modernized and the fabric changed to primarily rayon satin. The price increased to $1. If you're collecting, look for the black ones; they are the rarest. (High Noon collection)

Pre-1930 cowgirl outfits. The orange and black wool suit with leather buckle was worn by Juanita Howell. The red wool suit with white goatskin applique and fringe was made and worn by Mary Parks, famous bronc rider. The blue and red suit with crewelwork design and silk collar was worn by Vaughn K. Huskey, famous trick and bronc rider, who was also the first woman to bulldog a steer from the running board of a car. (National Cowgirl Hall of Fame collection)

27

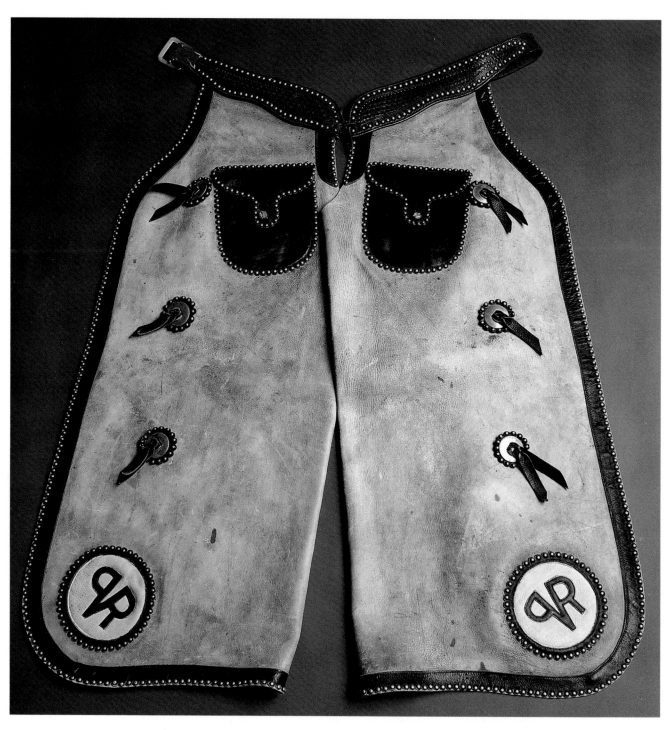

*H*orsehide chaps embellished with nickel conchas and studs. The circles hold either the wearer's initials or ranch brand. (Tyler and Teresa Beard collection)

A group of Wild West showmen in the late 1920s. Notice the beaded Indian vests, big hats, and trousers tucked into their fancy boots. There are no western belt buckles, and no piped western yokes. The brightly colored satin print shirts lost their popularity in the mid-1930s. But today rodeo cowboys are wearing psychedelic shirts reminiscent of this early style. (Photo courtesy Tyler Beard)

A group of rodeo gals in the 1920s. Most of their outfits have been homemade. Before the early 1930s, classic western designs were still in their infancy—no arrow pockets or pearl snaps here. Sateen shirts were becoming very popular, oversized silk bandanas knotted low in the front, and jodhpurs or riding bloomers were acceptable by the mid-1920s. Oversized hats were expected. Most of these cowgirls are wearing chaps and spurs, and the cowgirl boots were worn almost exclusively by the late 1920s, replacing English-style riding boots, and rubberized and canvas suede booties. (Photo courtesy Pro Rodeo Cowboy Association)

1930–1970
NASHVILLE MEETS HOLLYWOOD: THE GOLDEN YEARS OF WESTERN WEAR

Tom Mix was born in Pennsylvania in 1880. He went west to work with Colonel Zack Mulhall's Wild West Show. In 1906 he joined the Miller Brothers' 101 Wild West Show, where he worked hard to become a world-class champion rodeo cowboy. Tom was a saddle dandy, but also a talented, hard-working actor and cowboy who did all his own stunts. (Photo National Cowboy Hall of Fame)

The main catalyst that spurred western wear further into popularity in the '30s, '40s, and '50s, was the growing tourist industry. Automobile and train travel were becoming widely accessible. Now people could see the West and attend events such as the Texas Centennial World's Fair (1936), Cheyenne Frontier Days, the Pendleton Round-up, the Calgary Stampede, and the Grand Ole Opry.

Will Rogers, early cowboy philosopher and rope-trick artist deluxe, was America's most revered performer of the time. Gene Autry, Roy Rogers, the Lone Ranger and Tonto, Red Rider, Hopalong Cassidy, and other silver-screen idols rode through the 1940s and '50s, influencing western wear along the way. These stars and other singing cowboys were the first to bring heavily embroidered shirts, ornate and flashy boots, decorative belts and intricate buckles, and colorful neckerchiefs to western wear. It was during this period that Nashville discovered the Hollywood cowboy.

On the family scene, dude-ranch vacations were extremely popular. If you didn't have a car, the Santa Fe Railroad would take you out West. To go on one of these vacations, you absolutely had to dude up. Because of this, western wear was becoming an industry. Popular since the late 1920s, western-wear catalogs were an answer to this

Singer Skeets Yaney wore this late-1940s Rodeo Ben creation of cream-and-black checkered wool with appliqued leaf and quarter-note designs, and black arrows with cord lacing and black piping. (Country Music Hall of Fame collection)

growing demand. In the '30s, catalogs were showing calfskin and fringe vests and jackets for men and women, a wide array of tall- and short-top boots in bright colors with fancy inlays, bandanas and silk scarves in an endless variety of colors with scarf slides and tie holders. Saddle jackets and pants of heavy canvas duck and jodhpurs were still in style. Sateen two-toned shirts with buttons and flap pockets were just beginning to show the western angles, and extended shirt cuffs now had six or more buttons. Fish brand slickers were still being offered; Pendleton coats and blanket-vests for men and women were commonplace; The lace-up Buck Jones shirt was a big seller; and a Levi jacket or jeans cost only two dollars.

Gloves and gauntlets were still being made in a variety of skins, with and without fringe. The fabrics used to make western clothing in the 1930s and '40s were gabardine, rayon, cotton, and wool. Cuffs and spurs had not changed much since the early 1900s; there were now just more varieties.

In chaps, the shotgun style had lost its popularity and the woolly was on the wane. Bat-wings remained popular and were getting even wider.

Hatbands that were beaded, made from horse hair or spotted with metal studs, and tooled-leather hat belts were becoming popular, replacing the wide silk and grosgrain bands of the '20s and '30s. All the popular hat styles that Stetson had made in the previous fifty years were still available. There were even hats named after famous personalities of the West, such as the "Bill Cody." Miller Hats were beginning to compete with Stetson, offering similar styles at lower prices. Narrow-brimmed dress hats, the forerunners of the "Open Road" of the 1950s and '60s, were beginning to appear.

N. TURK

Very little is actually known about Nathan Turk. In fact, in all my museum searching I could not even find a photograph of Turk or his shop that was on Ventura Boulevard in Los Angeles for over fifty years. He was truly the epitome of an Armenian Old World tailor—polite, soft-spoken, and a real gentleman. He could always be found in his small shop with his wife and son-in-law, Irving. "Nate always wore beautifully tailored western slacks, a shirt, and sometimes a full suit, but I never saw him wearing boots or a hat," said Irving.

Turk was crafting beautifully made garments in the 1920s, before his western clientele began to arrive in the 1930s. The western tailoring really took off when Turk began making equestrian and western outfits for riders in the Pasadena Rose Bowl Parades. The movie crowd began to blaze a trail to his door once they saw Tom Mix and Gene Autry wearing so many of Turk's outstanding embroidered shirts and suits.

When any of his peers speak of him, they remark on Turk's beautiful work. He was a perfectionist with immense pride in every garment that his shop produced. Like all the western tailors, he had a store in front of his shop, where you could buy off the rack some of the most incredible western outfits ever made. There is not one name in the country music world who did not own something by Turk. Mel Marion, who works for Resistol Hat Company, remembers a compliment that Nudie once paid Turk. Mel once visited Nudie in the hospital, and although Mel owned many clothes made by Nudie, he wore a Turk shirt that day. When he walked in, Nudie said, "Lean over here. I *thought* that was a Turk. We never *could* get our arrows that fine."

In 1977, due to poor health, N. Turk decided to retire. He first offered to sell his shop and contents to Nudie, who turned it down. He then offered it to Manuel. Having such respect for Mr. Turk, Manuel could not bring himself to put a price on this man's life's work. He gave Mr. Turk a blank check, but it was never cashed. As late as 1978, N. Turk was still in business, taking orders for custom western wear at his shop and through the mail. I could find no information about Turk beyond 1978. (If you have any information about N. Turk after this date, please contact the author through the publisher.)

Henry Maddox wore this stage costume by N. Turk in the 1940s. (Country Music Hall of Fame collection)

The famous Rose suit by N. Turk for Rose Maddox was made in the 1940s. This is one of the most incredible western stage outfits to ever come down the pike. (Country Music Hall of Fame collection)

Rodeo as an entertainment sport was just about the most exciting thing around. The public had gone hog-wild with rodeo fever everywhere. Cowgirls such as Tad Lucas—trick rider and eight-time all-round cowgirl champion at Madison Square Garden—and Lucyle Richards, world champion saddle bronc rider and trick rider, both had vast wardrobes through the 1940s.

Always in the spotlight, these cowgirls and dozens like them influenced what women wore in western wear.

After John Wayne appeared in buckskin and beads in *The Big Trail* (1930), he returned to his classic cowboy duds in 1939 when he made *Stagecoach*. Throughout the 1930s and '40s, western movies probably had more to do with creating the western-wear

THE SATURDAY EVENING POST

An Illustrated Weekly
Founded A.D. 1728 by Benj. Franklin

NRA
CODE

5c. the Copy   JUNE 29, 1935
10c. in Canada

GEORGE S. BROOKS · JACK DEMPSEY · ALVA JOHNSTON

By 1935 national magazines such as The Saturday Evening Post were publishing articles about the dude-ranch vacation craze and the obsession the entire country had with the West and all things western.

market and establishing western as a style than any other influence. We saw in these westerns exaggerated western yokes; arrow pockets; whipcord piping; the revival of the bib-front shirt, fancy embroidery, and snap-up fasteners on shirts.

A child's complete western outfit in the 1940s included: cuffs, chaps, rope, hat, shirt, vest, boots, spurs and straps, holster, play pistol, a pair of Levis, belt, and bandana. These could all be purchased for less than $30.

The noticeable addition to western wear in the mid to late 1940s, were leather and suede skirts, vests, and jackets. Western trousers for women were readily available after World War II. Hand-tooled belts for

men and women, trophy buckles, and ranger sets were suddenly available in hundreds of variations. Western jewelry—earrings, tie bars, cuff links, rings, and watchbands—was becoming more popular. By the late 1940s, the bolo tie appeared.

The first zip-up jeans for women were invented by Wrangler in 1948. About the same time, the classic cotton chambray and denim shirts, with the new metal-rim pearl snap buttons, hit the market.

By 1950 Nashville had all but abandoned the hillbilly look of flood-water pants, ill-fitting suits, and polka dot ties. It had embraced the singing-cowboy image and given him a suit jacket, more rhinestones, more embroidery, and brighter colors for the stage. Television was the great proponent of western wear in the '50s, as Gene Autry, Hopalong Cassidy, and Roy Rogers flickered across the screens in clothes the whole family could wear.

In the '50s, western clothing crossed all gender boundaries more than in any previous decade. Jackets, vests, hats, belts, buckles, even spurs and chaps were all made basically the same for both sexes. Hats in this time period had severe turned-up brims and lower, flatter crowns than ever before. The tall crowns and wider, flat brims took a back seat until the 1980s. Boots were made in a variety of styles and colors unimaginable only a few years before. A leftover from the

1940s were the wide box toes, but by 1957 the cockroach-killer toe had its foot in the corner.

Local and national country-music shows popped up all over the country, and dozens of television westerns portrayed their version of the West with clothing that was not always historically accurate. Some of the best-remembered shows were "Death Valley Days," "Rawhide," "Davy Crockett," "Bat Masterson," "Palladin," "Gunsmoke," "The Rifleman," and finally "Bonanza."

The blue-jeans craze started in the late 1950s. Men, women, and children were all wearing jeans and jean jackets. Nothing is more American than Levis, the pants which won the West and East of all hemispheres. In part, this trend was brought on by the bobbysoxers and James Dean and Marlon Brando, who starred in youth-oriented and motorcycle-cult films. When John Wayne starred in *The Searchers* in 1956, this movie had a profound impact on the public. (Even

in the '90s, the Duke continues to have a subliminal impact on the male species and his western wardrobe.) The Duke's famous line from the movie, "That'll be the day," inspired Buddy Holly to write the song of the same title.

By the end of the '50s, when the words *space age* began to appear in western-wear ads, the golden age of western wear was coming to an end. Manufacturers raved about the new man-made wonder fabrics when polyester infiltrated the world of denim. By 1966 permanent-press fabric had arrived, proclaiming that "the wrinkle is dead." Through Koratron's oven-baked process, denims were "pressed for life." Then the British pop invasion had western-wear companies baffled, not knowing how to hold onto their segment of the clothing market. Before they could effectively assimilate the mod era into western wear, they ran smack dab into the hippy movement.

Dime novels, pulps, and cowboy comics fed the imaginations of western enthusiasts. Physical descriptions, heroes, heroines, and outlaws, along with beautiful cover art, helped shape the trends in western wear in the years before 1950.

Rodeo Ben was also known as Ben, The Rodeo Tailor. Born in Philadelphia in 1894, Ben was known all over the world for his rodeo and stage wear. As a young man, he worked for Strawbridge Clothiers and several other clothing companies. While selling fabrics for a mill, a request came in from a local store for fabrics in bright colors—chartreuse, aqua, and fuchsia. It turned out that the rodeo circus had just hit town and badly needed material for costumes. Ben not only found the fabric, but offered to make some of the costumes himself. The quality of work and attention to detail created a steady stream of rodeo and circus customers for Ben. In 1930 he opened his own storefront with a tailoring shop in back.

His son, Rodeo Ben, Jr., began to work with his father at age eighteen in 1936. Ben, Jr., recalls the store being called The East's Most Western Store. Although many others claim to have been the first to put snaps on western shirts, photographs dated 1933 show that Rodeo Ben was definitely the leader in this arena. Rockmount was the first manufacturer to use snaps on western shirts, in 1946. Ben, Jr., tells the story of his father witnessing a rodeo cowboy getting hung up on his saddle when the saddle horn lodged in an opening of his button-up shirt. Ben immediately thought of the snaps being used on gloves at the time: if snaps were put on shirts, they would easily come apart in the event of a rodeo accident. After using the metal glove snaps for a while, he contacted Rau Fastener Company (still in business) to fashion a fancier snap out of mother-of-pearl. The snap-up western shirt became a standard and remained popular through the 1970s. (Aside from a small percentage of men's shirts today, Wrangler uses the largest quantity of snaps on their denim work shirts.) However, in the 1990s, snaps are experiencing a revival on men's and women's western shirts.

By the late 1930s, it was well known that Rodeo Ben was the clothier to the Beau Brummell of the Wild West—Tom Mix. Large portions of Hopalong Cassidy's, Gene Autry's, and Roy Rogers's extensive wardrobes were supplied by Ben. Ben, Jr., recalls that Roy and Gene had an agreement with his dad that he would never make the same outfit for both of them. When Gene Autry came out of the army in 1945, he was almost forty pounds thinner than when he went in. He asked Ben to close his shop to other customers while he created a whole new wardrobe for Gene.

The way Ben attracted much of his business was through the Madison Square Garden Rodeo. Each year he set up a temporary showroom and tailor shop at the Belvedere Hotel in New York City to accommodate all the cowgirls, cowboys, and celebrities who attended.

In 1947 Blue Bell, a manufacturer of dungarees and work overalls, approached Ben about designing an authentic cowboy-cut pair of jeans suitable for riding a horse, a bull, or any other critter in comfort. World-champion all-round cowboy, Jim Shoulders, worked with Ben and Blue Bell to help them understand just what a cowboy needed. Ben created the first pair of five-pocket, straight-legged, fitted blue jeans targeted at rodeo cowboys. Cowboys liked the fitted appearance due to double-needle felled seams for rugged durability, flat copper rivets that would not rub on the saddle, deep front pockets for gloves or other working-cowboy necessities, and split double-reinforced back pockets designed to be tool-proof. The broken-twill denim process prevented the fabric from wrinkling as much when washed. Ben also moved the ever-present watch pocket from down inside the pocket well up to the waistband area, which meant a watch chain could more easily be attached to a belt loop for easy access to the time. The rise in the back end was higher so a cowboy didn't have to sit on his billfold. Jim Shoulders and Freckles Brown test-rode Ben's prototype jeans. In 1947, after thirteen variations, the 13MWZ (thirteen tries, men's western zipper) was born. The 13MWZ was also the first pair of blue jeans with a zipper fly; before this, all closures fastened with buttons. The employees of Blue Bell were all asked to submit a name for the new blue jeans, and from these, the name Wranglers was chosen. Rodeo Ben became so well known that for years his face appeared, along with those of five champion rodeo cowboys, on all the paper tags stapled to the back pocket of Wrangler jeans.

Rodeo Ben put out several mail-order catalogs for the general public through the 1950s and remained in business in Philadelphia for nearly sixty years. In 1979, at age 92, Rodeo Ben, Sr., passed away. He was buried in his favorite pure-white western-cut suit. Rodeo Ben, Jr., kept the shop going until 1983, when health problems made it necessary for him to close the business.

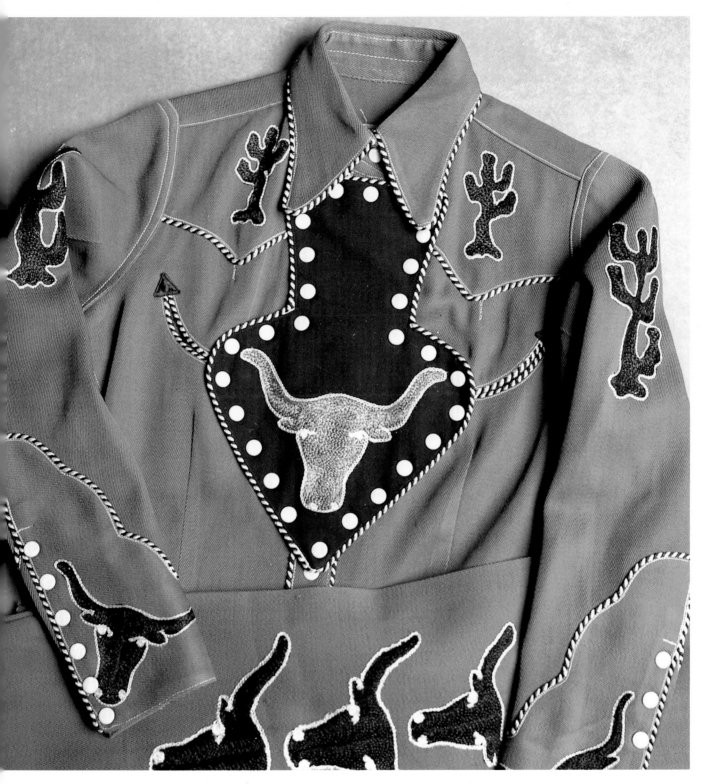

A fine example of a 1940s Rodeo Ben suit, now worth $1,500. Kelly green wool with longhorns all over the place, early painted snaps on the cuffs, and an unusual bib shape. This same suit style was still in Ben's catalog in the 1950s. (Tyler and Teresa Beard collection)

*R*odeo Ben must
have had a time
concentrating on this
fuchsia silk-satin shirt
with multiple Indian
heads and full feather
headdresses in chain-
stitch embroidery,
made for Gene Autry
in the 1940s. (The
Gene Autry Western
Heritage Museum
collection)

A Rodeo Ben shirt
worn by Gene
Autry featured wavy
"smiles," also known
as arrow pockets, with
topstitching around
the cuffs, collar, and
pearl-snap placket.
The embroidery
designs on this 1940s
shirt are reminiscent
of Indian petroglyphs.
(The Gene Autry
Western Heritage
Museum collection)

*P*hotos of Patsy Montana and Gene Autry in Chicago, 1930, between performances on the National Barn Dance radio show. This is a rare picture of Gene before he went to Hollywood. Patsy is known the world over for having been the first female to have a number-one country song, "I Wannna Be a Cowboy's Sweetheart." (Photos Country Music Hall of Fame)

*D*on Maddox wore this chain-stitch embroidered suit onstage with sister Rose. *The red wool gabardine with matching satin shirt were designed by N. Turk. The Maddoxes had outstanding stage wear which has been collected, but nobody seems to know where their boots are. If you find them, call Tyler Beard. (Country Music Hall of Fame collection)*

*R*ose Maddox had a flair for designing stage outfits, along with tailor N. Turk, that combined current fashion of the late 1930s and 1940s with a western touch, such as the purple leather fringe seen here. The chain embroidery is reminiscent of Scandinavian or Dutch folk art. (Photos by Richard Connors, private collection)

An unusual combination of colors on a 1940s bluebird boot by Olsen-Stelzer for Gene Autry. (The Gene Autry Western Heritage Museum collection)

Only two pairs of these boots are known to exist. The "Squash Blossom" boot, so named because of the design on the boots with a naja in the front and the rear, resembles a turquoise necklace. This boot appeared in a mail-order catalog offered by the Las Cruces Boot Company. The engraved sterling silver toe tips were added later. (The Gene Autry Western Heritage Museum collection)

GENE AUTRY

Gene Autry is the richest cowboy in the world. Autry starred in over ninety films from 1935–55. He also made hundreds of records beginning in 1929. From 1950–55, he made ninety-one episodes of his highly successful television show. In the late 1950s, Gene retired from the western hoopla to manage his business ventures—radio stations, newspapers, oil wells, cattle ranches, flying schools, a traveling rodeo, publishing companies, a baseball team, and a chain of movie theaters.

Gene Autry was a class act all the way. He only bought the best, which is attested by the fact that he was voted one of the ten best-dressed men in America in 1950. Bohlin made Gene's silver and gold jewelry, belt buckles, and belts. When traveling, Gene carried his hats in hand-tooled luggage with sterling and gold buckles and latches. In the past, Stetson made all of his hats, but currently Resistol custom makes the original style just for Gene.

By 1950 a large portion of Gene's Hollywood home was being used as closet space. Hundreds of multicolored, custom, inlaid boots by Lucchese, Rios, Olsen-Stelzer, and Charlie Garrison lined the walls. Stetson hat boxes in rows were stacked to the ceiling, and closets burst at the hinges full of hundreds of embroidered shirts and suits in an array of colors, styles, and designs that solidified Gene's position as top-dog clothes horse in the world of western wear.

Although Gene owned garments by every western tailor, Rodeo Ben of Philadelphia was his favorite. Ben used fine gabardine, whipcord, flannel, and twill cut in a myriad of western designs. All of Gene's tuxedos were western-cut, and he even had golf boots with cleats, made by Lucchese. He wore a neckerchief or a hand-painted four-in-hand tie with a large double knot.

From his early days, Gene Autry had a dream to open a museum whose main focus was on the people who settled the West—everyday people as well as working cowboys, artists, authors, filmmakers, television and radio personalities. "I have always wanted to exhibit and interpret the heritage of the West, to show how it has influenced America and the world." Gene Autry spent $54 million, and in 1988 his dream was realized when the Gene Autry Western Heritage Museum opened.

Official Gene Autry Ranch Outfit sold in 1941. Only the hat is missing. (Photo courtesy The Gene Autry Western Heritage Museum collection)

*G*ene Autry wore a lot of cream and white suits by Rodeo Ben and Nudie. This one by Nudie was made in the 1940s and shows red piping all around with red snaps. The square-bib front boasts the Texas and American flags. The Nudie label visible inside the shirt was Nudie's original cowgirl in the buff (except for her ten-gallon hat, boots, and a holster). After Nudie got religion, the cowgirl also wore a bikini, then later a bolero vest and skirt. (The Gene Autry Western Heritage Museum collection)

*P*oor old Gene Autry, in the 1940s, just can't find anything to wear. (Courtesy The Gene Autry Western Heritage Museum)

Lucchese made these vibrant red calf boots with gray kangaroo collar, counter, and vamp overlays for Gene Autry in the 1940s. Flowers, arrows, vines, longhorns, even card suits combine nine colors, making an outstanding statement with an unlikely grouping of design elements. (The Gene Autry Western Heritage Museum collection)

Two urban cowgirls in the late 1940s, duded up and ready to tear up the town. Yeeeei-haaaa! (Photo National Cowboy Hall of Fame Museum)

*R*ed, white, and blue Rodeo Ben shirt in red gabardine and cotton
twill with three-snap spacing and candy-stripe whipcord trim.
(The Gene Autry Western Heritage Museum collection)

Benedictine gold and burgundy Lucchese boots with swirls and geometric configurations creates one spectacular piece of leather artistry. (The Gene Autry Western Heritage Museum collection)

Western-wear mail-order catalogs got their start in the mid-1920s and are still popular today. There was a time when most people had to order through the western-wear catalogs or Sears and Roebuck. These folks either lived in desolate rural areas, had no car, or lived in a state where western wear was not easily found. The arrival of a new catalog was an event; people would wear out the pages ogling and awing, trying to make up their minds what they could not live without. (Tyler and Teresa Beard collection)

48

Harlequin longhorn boots with fanciful diamond checkerboard effect, by Lucchese of San Antonio, Texas. (The Gene Autry Western Heritage Museum collection)

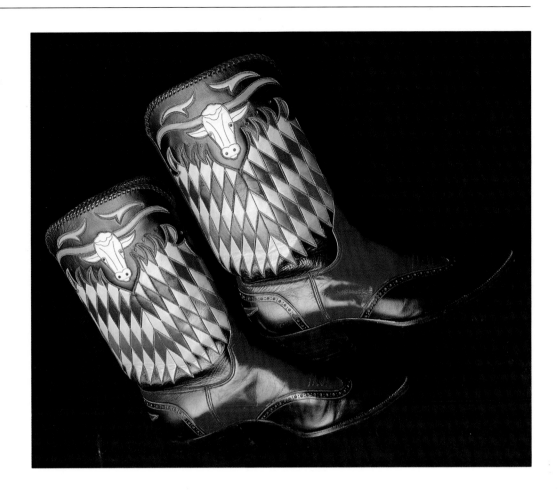

Rodeos, frontier days, parades, and square dances have always been a monumental force in perpetuating the craze for all things western, especially clothing and western-style entertainment. (Tyler and Teresa Beard collection)

VIOLA GRAE

There is even less information about Viola Grae than about Turk. We know that she was originally from Minnesota. Her business was in Los Angeles and was known primarily as an embroidery shop. Viola advertised heavily in rodeo programs all over the country, as did most of the western tailors.

Rex Bell, early singing cowboy star who was married to Clara Bow, owned a few western-wear stores after his career in music, and sold fancy western garb all embroidered by Viola Grae. N. Turk and Rodeo Ben of Philadelphia, along with lesser-known tailors from all over the country, would send much of their embroidery piecework to Viola. Manuel described Viola as "a lovely little blond woman, full of energy, piss, and vinegar who ran her shop with an iron fist." Viola kept her business going about thirty years. As late as 1966, she was still advertising in rodeo programs and *Western Horseman* magazine: "Elaborate jeweled embroidered clothing with thousands of aurora borealis rhinestones." She retired in the early 1970s. Manuel remembered going to visit her in a small apartment in Los Angeles in the mid-1980s. From there I have been unable to find further information about her. She was so respected in her field that much of her embroidery was signed with her name on the outside of the garment.

Before Nudie, in the early 1940s, N. Turk made all of Hank's stage wear, but Nudie of Hollywood made this unbelievable suit for Hank. Viola Grae embroidered the shirt to match the Humpty Dumpty boots. (By the way, Hank has lost track of his Golden Nugget suit. If anybody knows its whereabouts, contact Hank through the publisher.) (Photo Country Music Hall of Fame)

A collaboration between Charlie Garrison and Viola Grae resulted in unusual embroidery on the boot heel and quilt stitching all the way down the foot. (The Gene Autry Western Heritage Museum collection)

*In 1948 Hank Thompson had a big hit, "Humpty
Dumpty Heart." Figural theme embroidery,
especially pertaining to hit records, was something
Nudie, Rodeo Ben, Viola Grae, and N. Turk all
participated in. The boots were made at Nudie's
and the embroidery was executed by Viola Grae.
(Country Music Hall of Fame collection)*

51

A very sedate double-breasted Nudie suit with multi-arrow design is a western classic from the 1940s. The vibrant shirt, also by Nudie, shows fabric applique with red and blue rhinestones and the early recessed pearl snaps. (The Gene Autry Western Heritage Museum collection)

Three variations on a longhorn, by Lucchese. (The Gene Autry Western Heritage Museum collection)

This little cowpoke probably lived in New Jersey or some such place. Like a brushfire, every home in America was infiltrated by the neighborhood picture show, radio programs, and Saturday afternoon shoot-'em-up westerns. From 1930–1960, every boy and girl in the country was touched in some way by western mania. (Photo courtesy Tyler Beard)

It's easy to envision Gary Cooper or Randolph Scott in this 1940s Jantzen "Made for the Hollywood Stars" rare cowboy swimsuit. (Tyler and Teresa Beard collection)

Little buckarettes and buckaroos wore play outfits endorsed by their favorite western movie and TV heroines and heroes. (Photo courtesy The Gene Autry Western Heritage Museum collection)

*T*he Maddox Brothers—Ron, Fred, Cal, Don, and Henry—with their sister, Rose, were billed as "the most colorful hillbilly band in the land." They were known for their wild and woolly antics onstage, yelping and hollering and cutting up. Their music was half hillbilly, half rockabilly—before rockabilly was a recognized musical style. The last song the band recorded together before they split up in 1956 was "The Death of Rock 'N' Roll." Rose told me that N. Turk designed and made all of their clothing, and that Lucchese made all of their boots. Their Turk clothing was early 1940s style, but the Maddoxes wore the same clothes right through the 1950s. Sadly, all the brothers but Don are gone, but Rose performs with a new band which includes her grandson Donny. (Photo Country Music Hall of Fame)

*L*ucchese Boots made a series of T. O. Pride boots from the hide of a grand champion steer by the same name. The steer was purchased for $44,000, and upon his death in 1945, more than fifteen pairs of boots were made from his hide. Most of the boots were bought by celebrities for a staggering $3,500 a pair! (The Gene Autry Western Heritage Museum collection)

The red floral embroidered shirt in the background is homemade from a popular store-bought pattern. The tan shirt with a cowboy on a horse, roping a bronc, is an off-the-rack Frontex. The two shiny numbers are: a fuchsia silk-satin 1950s Nudie shirt with horse heads and a cowboy on a horse with a rhinestone lariat; a gold 1930s cotton-satin Miller Stockman catalog shirt with embroidered cowboy on a bucking bronc (this style remained in their catalog through the 1950s). (Courtesy The Rainbow Man)

*T*urk made this fire-engine red musical-note suit for one of the Maddox brothers. The symmetry is perfect, and the western belt loops and rear-pocket yokes are unusual and ornate with embroidery and rhinestones. (Photo by Richard Connors, private collection)

Pinup cowgirls were used on calendars and billboards, in magazines ads, and they made public appearances to sell literally everything from the 1940s to the 1960s. There were eight Pangburn Chocolate cowgirls, each for a different assortment. Pangburn Chocolates is still operating in Fort Worth, Texas. (Tyler and Teresa Beard collection)

As late as the 1950s and '60s, advertisers relied on western nostalgia depicting romantic scenes of the Old West in order to sell their products. In the 1970s and '80s, the trend was reversed. In the '90s once again the romance of the Old West is being used to sell everything from investment portfolios to barbecue sauce. (Photo courtesy Stetson Hats)

Rodeo Ben, Jr., is on the front of this mail-order catalog from the 1950s. Inside you could order your heart's desire with Rodeo Ben classics from the '30s, '40s, and '50s. The Rodeo Bens ran a complete tack, saddle, and western-wear store in Philadelphia for more than fifty years. (Tyler and Teresa Beard collection)

"CHUCK WAGON" by Melbourne Brindle

Naturally they're STETSON HATS

*A*side from the purple silk "Let 'Er Buck" scarf in the center (1920–40), the rest of these scarves are from the 1940s–60s. This is a fraction of a collection owned by Jack Pressler.

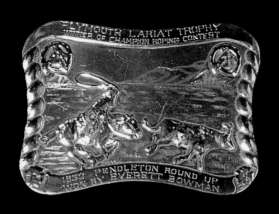

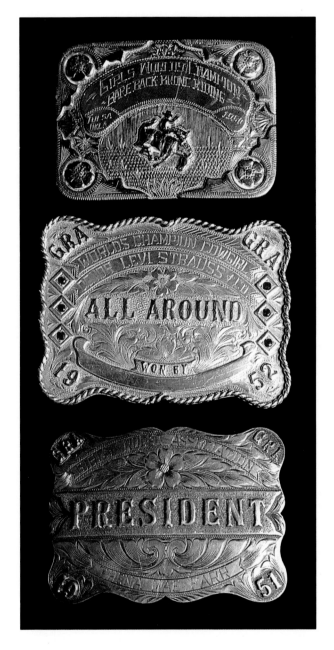

Winning trophy buckles for rodeo events became popular in the 1920s for men and women. Pre-1950s trophy buckles have become highly collectible, especially bearing names like Casey Tibbs. (Facing page: National Cowboy Hall of Fame collection, this page: National Cowgirl Hall of Fame)

Rodeo cowgirls began to put their names on chaps and spurs mainly after 1945. (The National Cowgirl Hall of Fame collection)

Hank Williams, "King of the Honky-Tonks," wearing a Nudie musical-note suit, which he popularized and is famous for. His boots, made by Dixon Boot Company, Wichita Falls, Texas, also had musical staffs and two-toned leather notes that matched his suits. When Hank died in 1953, his song "I'll Never Get Out of This World Alive" was on the charts. (Photo Country Music Hall of Fame)

Roy always had a flair for stage wear. Back in the 1930s, when he was singing with the Sons of the Pioneers, he thought the boys needed to spruce up a mite. Roy himself made leather vests laced around the edges, with Sons of the Pioneers burned in like a brand on the vest backs. He was always sewing leather fringe or doodads on their costumes.

Roy made thirty-six films without Dale between 1938 and 1942, and they costarred in scores of films together. By the mid-1950s, Roy and Dale had made 107 episodes of "The Roy Rogers Show" for television.

Prior to World War II, Roy mainly wore studio costumes, store-bought western wear, and some custom clothing from Rodeo Ben. It was not until after Gene Autry went into the service that Roy was proclaimed "King of the Cowboys" by the publicity department at Republic Pictures. With the budget increases, Roy's wardrobe began to explode. After his first pictures in 1944 with Dale Evans, her rootin'-tootin' performance earned her the title "Queen of the West." Through the 1940s, their western wardrobes were made by Rodeo Ben and N. Turk; some outfits were from studio wardrobe; and every once in a while you could catch them wearing an off-the-rack H Bar C, Frontex, or Rockmount embroidered shirt.

Roy wore out hundreds of double-eagle boots, mostly made for him by Hyer Boot Company in Olathe, Kansas, and Nudie of Hollywood. He told me that every boot maker in the country would send him free pairs of boots. If they didn't fit, he'd pull out his pocketknife and slice along the edge to give his toes some breathing room.

Roy only changed his hat crease once during his career, from a higher, pinched crease to his own version of the "horseshoe" crease, which rises in the front of the crown almost to a point. Roy demonstrated to me how he still creases his own hats, adding that nobody else can do it the way he likes. "Stetson used to make all of my hats. Now Resistol makes 'em, but I have to crease 'em myself."

Bohlin of Hollywood made most of their belts, buckles, spurs, and hatbands throughout their careers.

It is evident that Dale loved stars; they can be seen on just about everything she wore between 1945 and 1955. Although early on Dale wore some pants with embroidered shirts, she really stuck with skirts, shirts, and vests. She wore a wide variety of hats during her career. Dale's boots were usually store-bought or from the companies such as Gold Bond and others that she and Roy endorsed. Dale usually had the makers add stars to her boots.

By the early 1950s, Roy was thinking of ways to glitz up their outfits. When Roy and Dale were making more public appearances in huge stadiums and rodeo arenas. Roy said he "wanted the kids to be able to see them better." Nudie, who had been making clothing for the "King and Queen," solved the problem with rhinestones and more fringe, which reflected light and waved in the breeze as the performers rode in on Trigger and Buttermilk. From that point on, Nudie made the majority of Dale and Roy's clothing. Even today, Roy only wears western clothing. The day we met him at the Roy Rogers and Dale Evans Museum in Victorville, California, he was wearing black western slacks, an embroidered H Bar C shirt, a gold Bohlin horseshoe bolo tie, his ever-present white hat, gold Bohlin western rings and watchband, and a pair of store-bought black boots (he said, "I picked up five pairs of them somewhere in Oklahoma.")

Happy trails to Roy, Dale, Dusty, and the whole family.

(Photo courtesy Roy Rogers and Dale Evans Museum)

*D*ale Evans,
"Queen of the
West." (Photo courtesy
Roy Rogers and Dale
Evans Museum)

*T*he Happy Hunting
Ground"—a Roy
Rogers and Dale Evans
closet full of Nudie.
(Roy Rogers and Dale
Evans Museum
collection)

In Hollywood, Edward H. Boblin made the parade saddles for the stars. These saddles today are worth from $5,000 to $150,000. His catalogs featured saddles, tack, spurs, belts, buckles, chaps, vests, skirts, and anything a little cowboy or cowgirl heart desired. This is Roy Rogers about 1950. (Photo Country Music Hall of Fame)

The Rose Bowl Parade in Pasadena, California, is one big foofaraw of western-wear foppery and equestrian pageantry, unequaled anywhere this side of Mexico City. These boots were made for Roy Rogers specifically for the Rose Bowl Parades and were probably made by Charlie Garrison in the late 1950s. The engraved sterling and 10K gold wingtips and heel guards were added later. (Roy Rogers and Dale Evans Museum collection)

This Indian-head shirt, made by Nudie in the 1950s for Roy Rogers, is what western-wear dreams are made of. (Roy Rogers and Dale Evans Museum collection)

Roy Rogers loved Bullet, the wonder dog, so much that he had Nudie memorialize him in rhinestones. (Roy Rogers and Dale Evans Museum collection)

Nudie Cohn was born Nudka Cohn in Kiev, Russia, in 1902. His father was a poor boot maker. When Nudie was eleven years old, his family immigrated to the United States. Nudie got his famous name at immigration, not in Hollywood, when his name was misspelled on entrance papers.

Nudie worked a variety of jobs in Brooklyn before moving to California at age sixteen to pursue a boxing career. At nineteen, he began getting non-speaking extra parts in movies in Hollywood. To earn more money, Nudie began about 1926 whipping up costumes on an individual-order basis. One of his customers was Gloria Swanson, but he was still always broke. Nudie decided in 1928 to hitchhike across the country back to Brooklyn to visit his family. In Mankato, Minnesota, Nudie met Bobbie, his future wife, and the next six years of his life are a little sketchy. We do know that for a while he sewed lingerie for a women's garment company in New York City. He also made specialty costumes and G-strings for strippers. Some say this is where the name Nudie came from, but he was actually using the name before this time.

In 1934 Nudie and Bobbie married. With $300 between them, they returned to Mankato to open a tailor shop. In 1940 they sold the shop for $2,700 and moved to Los Angeles. Nudie worked in a few tailor shops, sewed more G-strings, and was beginning to notice that western tailoring was up and coming in Los Angeles. N. Turk had been in Los Angeles for at least fifteen years before Nudie, doing conventional tailoring, making equestrian riding gear, and doing cowboy tailoring for Tom Mix, Ken Maynard, and other stars. Viola Grae also had opened a Los Angeles shop and was making custom garments and doing light embroidery, which was her specialty.

It didn't take long before the celebrity hot line sent Nudie lots of customers. In those early days, Tex Williams, Hank Thompson, Roy Rogers, Gene Autry, Audie Murphy, Dale Evans, Jock Mahoney, Guy Madison, Dale Robertson, and Spade Cooley, just to name a few, kept him busy. But Nudie still always seemed to be broke. It was Tex Williams who gave Nudie a horse and saddle to auction for $150 to get his first sewing machine. This enabled Nudie to set up shop in his garage.

Once again Tex gave Nudie his second big break when he asked Nudie to make costumes for his band. Nudie took the measurements and recited them to his assistant, who was not entirely sober at the time. Leg lengths got chest measurements, and the short of it was that none of the costumes fit! Nudie had to remake all of them. Nobody seems to remember what they looked like, but they created a sensation at the Palace Barn, where the group was performing. The next night, 2,500 people showed up (the usual crowd was less than 400). Tex was so happy he gave Nudie the full $750 he owed him for the suits, and Nudie was so overwhelmed with the money and the crowd's reaction that he went into the men's room and fainted.

This was really the beginning of Nudie's success. His customer list increased, and so did his prices. For the first time, Nudie was not broke. His first shop that was open to the public opened in 1947, and Nudie's of Hollywood was born. In the late 1940s and throughout the 1950s, Nudie turned out thousands of garments for his following, which included newer customers Hank Snow, Little Jimmy Dickens, Hank Williams, Ernest Tubb, Cowboy Copas, Hopalong Cassidy, Jay Silverheels, Lash LaRue, Hoot Gibson, Merle Travis, Lefty Frizzell, Gail Davis, Glenn Ford, Edward G. Robinson, and countless others.

Throughout Nudie's career, he continued making costumes for the movies, mainly westerns. John Wayne had clothing made by him, and Nudie said, "The Duke wore working-cowboy clothes, nothing fancy." Nudie always retained his customers who simply wanted fine-tailored clothing.

Another of Nudie's famous customers was Colonel Parker, Elvis's manager. There are more than three versions explaining why Nudie made Elvis's 24K gold lamé rhinestone suit. All that is certain is that he did make it, and the cost was $10,000. The only reason a suit would cost that much in the late 1950s would be for publicity. Nudie said his profit was about $9,500. Elvis and Nudie both got well-deserved mileage out of that suit.

In the 1960s, Nudie added to his clients such notables as Mel Tillis, Freddie Hart, Buck Owens, Ronald Reagan, Conway Twitty, George Jones and Tammy Wynette, Diana Ross, Michael Jackson, Liberace, Elton John, The Rolling Stones, The Beatles, Merle Haggard, Twiggy, Marty Robbins, Johnny Cash, The Grateful Dead, Clint Eastwood, Porter Wagoner, Dolly Parton, Judy Lynn, The Riders of the Purple Sage, and the Flying Burrito Brothers (Graham Parsons's famous suit had nude women embroidered on the lapels and marijuana leaves embroidered all over the suit in technicolor).

Rose Clements was Nudie's master embroiderer beginning in the mid-1960s. In England she had received a master's scholarship in embroidery, and when she came to Los Angeles she brought her own embroidery machines. Rose is the one woman in the United States who has the know-how and talent to use machines that will produce the Swiss, chain, and satin stitches. Rose, now in her early seventies, works in her home in Los Angeles, still producing embroidery for Nudie's.

By the late 1960s, Nudie had become a living legend, a folk hero to both young and old in California. The shop has been listed on Los Angeles tour guide maps as a site since the 1970s. Nudie crossed all the boundaries of fashion. He influenced the western-wear industry for nearly forty years. In 1984, at age 81, Nudie succumbed to cancer. More than eight hundred people attended the funeral—all wearing Nudie clothes. Dale Evans gave the eulogy, and "I'm Headed for the Last Roundup" was sung in Nudie's honor. His famous white Cadillac, decorated with pistol door handles, silver-dollar-embedded leather upholstery, topped off by longhorns mounted on the hood, was parked out front. Nudie's is still open and making duds for country music and rock 'n' roll stars. Nudie's wife, Bobbie Cohn, and one of their two granddaughters, Jamie Cohn Barragan, run the shop in its original location in North Hollywood. To this day, the Rose Bowl Parade crowd goes to Nudie's, which has been in business for more than forty-six years.

Country music would never have been the same without Nudie, and the golden age of western wear might not have been. Thanks, Nudie, the original Rhinestone Cowboy.

*H*ank Thompson was one red-hot, ding-dong daddy from Dumas in this crimson leather jacket with silver metallic leather and rhinestones by Nudie, early 1950s. (Country Music Hall of Fame collection)

*J*immy C. Newman, "The Cajun," a Grand Ole Opry regular, dropped these late-1950s Nudie suit pants off at Manuel's for alterations in 1993. (The Cajun collection)

*R*ay Price in the 1950s sporting a Nudie smoke-signals suit with leather shoulder and sleeve fringe. (Photo Country Music Hall of Fame)

__M__erle Travis (left) and Hank Thompson in the early 1950s, strutting their western stuff. (Photo Country Music Hall of Fame)

BUCK OWENS

Buck Owens and his Buckaroos wore Nudie suits throughout the 1960s. Buck had fifteen number-one hits between 1958 and 1992. The "Buck Owens Ranch" television show was syndicated with over 100 stations between 1966 and 1973, and Owens was seen as a regular on "Hee Haw" between 1969 and 1986. He popularized the honky-tonk freight-train style, which still influences rock and country musicians today. (Photo courtesy Buck Owens Productions)

LITTLE JIMMY DICKENS

Little Jimmy Dickens started out in radio, like so many other Nashville performers. Novelty songs became his trademark, some of which made reference to his diminutive stature—less than five feet in boots. But Little Jimmy is big onstage.

Better known around Nashville as "Tater" (for his hit record "Take an Old Cold Tater and Wait"), Jimmy became a member of the Grand Ole Opry in 1948. He became close friends with Hank Williams while on a European tour of air bases organized by the Grand Ole Opry in 1949, and they remained fishing and hunting buddies until Hank's death. In 1951 he was the first ever to wear a Nudie rhinestone suit at the Grand Ole Opry and was practically laughed off the stage. In that same year, Hank and Audrey Williams opened their own western-wear store, Hank and Audrey's Corral, introducing Nudie to Nashville. Soon after, rhinestones became a staple of the country music community. In 1964 Little Jimmy became the first country performer to make a world tour.

True to his hit record "I'm Little But I'm Loud," Jimmy appears on the Grand Ole Opry regularly, and when he's not performing, he greets visitors at Opryland USA. Tater continues to wow audiences with his explosive and dynamic performances. Jimmy, you may be little, but you're big on heart and soul. Suit by Manuel (1992); matching boots by Bo Riddle (1992).

Little Jimmy Dickens had many guitar suits made. Nudie combined chain-stitch embroidery, rhinestones, and leather-fringed yokes and shoulders. (Little Jimmy Dickens collection)

Guitar suit made by Nudie in the 1950s for Little Jimmy Dickens. Suits like this worn by celebrities can now fetch as much as $4,000 on the collector's market. (Country Music Hall of Fame collection)

*T*ater's big hit "May the Bird of Paradise Fly Up Your Nose" prompted Nudie to make a series of various bird-theme suits. (Little Jimmy Dickens collection)

*I*n the 1940s and '50s, most successful country-band members wore identical matching outfits. The lead man would sometimes dress differently to set himself apart. This photograph is Hank Thompson and the Brazos Valley Boys. The band was voted top country-western band by the trade magazines from 1953–66. Suits by Nudie. (Photo Country Music Hall of Fame)

HANK SNOW

In the early years of his career, Hank Snow mainly wore suits and ties with dress shirts that were store-bought and conservative. Canadian-born Snow moved to the United States and joined the Grand Ole Opry after his record "I'm Movin' On" topped the charts. In the late 1950s Hank began to develop his personal style. He wore short-waisted jackets, usually with two, one, or no buttons at all. He still wore plain dress shirts with various string, bolo, and bow ties, and in all my searching, I could only find one photograph from 1944 of Hank ever wearing a cowboy hat. Hank was introduced to Nudie in the late 1950s, who from then on made all of his clothing, except for a few suits by Harvey Krantz in the 1970s. (Krantz, at age 64, is still tailoring western clothes and costumes in Calabasas, California.) Hank's embroidered and rhinestoned suits were covered with figural themes such as frogs, birds, clipper ships, stagecoaches, Indian heads, and I assume anything that struck his fancy. James Leddy, in Abilene, Texas, has been making Hank's belts and boots for the last thirty years, and from the '60s on, Hank has continued to wear his Nudie suits.

Hank Snow in one of Nudie's popular Indian-theme shirts and pants. The large collar suggests late 1960s style. (Photo Country Music Hall of Fame)

A yellow and gold Nudie suit with headdresses on the sleeves, sterling-silver buckle pockets, with piped arrows on the trousers and jacket. Multi-colored thunderbirds and Northwest Indian totem poles are meticulously embroidered solidly down each leg. The entire suit is dotted with rhinestones. Made for Hank Snow between 1960 and 1965. (Courtesy of Hank Snow and The Grand Ole Opry Museum at Opryland USA)

*B*right pink suit made for Hank Snow by Nudie between 1955 and 1960, has rhinestone lapels and what I call the "Empty Fishpond" design: there are no fish, just frogs, lily pads, and a giant bird on the back. The outfit is topped off by a red velvet bow tie. (Courtesy of Hank Snow and The Grand Ole Opry Museum at Opryland USA)

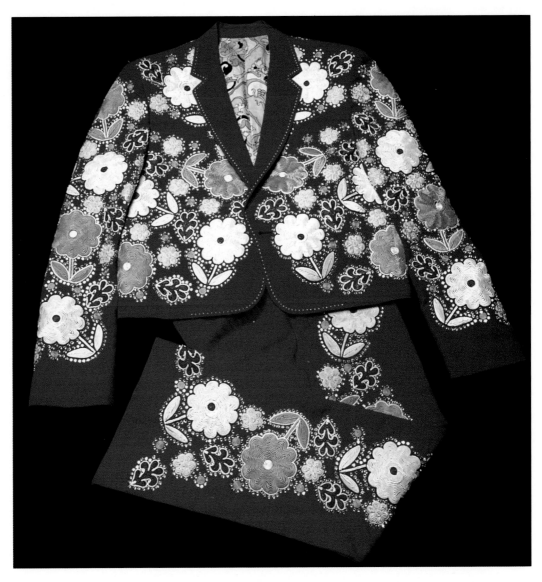

P*lum-colored suit with massive flower design in wavelike embroidery
patterns that resemble early Chinese kimonos. Made by Nudie in the 1970s.
(Collection of The Grand Ole Opry Museum at Opryland USA)*

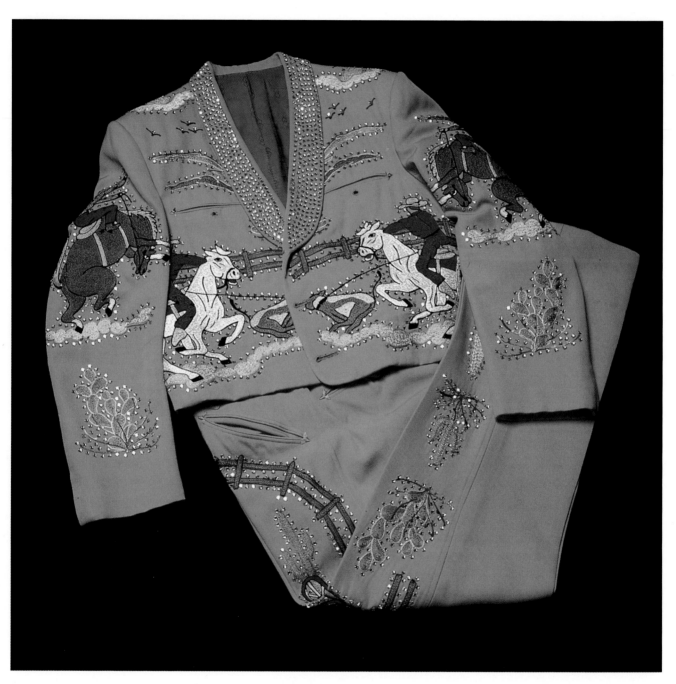

A Nudie wagon-train suit complete with oxen, split-rail fences, cacti, cowboys on broncs, and roping calves—all in a snow-capped mountain valley of embroidery and rhinestones. Note the strait arrow pockets, which were not seen as much as curves and half-circles. Made for Hank Snow between 1955 and 1965, (Courtesy of Hank Snow and The Grand Ole Opry Museum at Opryland USA)

A *1960s bright orange suit with gold metallic thread in a jigsaw puzzle design that covers the entire suit. Multicolored embroidered floral designs weave their way through the gold thread. The entire suit is accented by sterling-silver jacket buttons and western buckle sets on the jacket cuffs. Made by Nudie, 1960s. (Collection of The Grand Ole Opry Museum at Opryland USA)*

In the 1950s, Webb Pierce had over twenty number-one hits. When Hank Williams died, Webb became the heir-apparent to the honky-tonk throne. One of his biggest hits, "I'm In the Jailhouse Now," prompted Webb to have Nudie make him this jailhouse suit. Notice that the arrow sign on Webb's right leg says "To Nudie's." (Photo Country Music Hall of Fame)

REX ALLEN

Rex Allen, the "Arizona Cowboy," with his wonder horse Koko, thrilled millions of fans in movies and rodeo appearances. Rex began his career in rodeo about 1939, then in the late 1940s a call from Hollywood brought Rex to Republic Studios, where he became the last in a long line of singing cowboys. Following in the boot-steps of Roy Rogers, Rex Allen emulated the "King of the Cowboys" in his appearance. Roy introduced Rex to Nudie in the mid-1950s; the rest is western-wear history. Nudie of Hollywood tailored the majority of Rex's wardrobe after that time, from hats to suits to boots. Tony Lama Boot Company and Bailey Hats later on hired Rex to endorse their products.

Rex Allen, "the Arizona Cowboy," made a string of B-westerns and was very popular in parades and rodeos as a celebrity guest for another twenty years after he retired from the screen. Rex is alive and well today in Arizona.

Gold lamé suit by Nudie, 1960s. (Photo courtesy of Rex Allen)

The gang's all here at Nudie's, early 1950s, left to right: Tex Williams (who loaned Nudie the money to open his shop in 1946), Gene Autry, Nudie, Roy Rogers, Rex Allen. (Photo Country Music Hall of Fame)

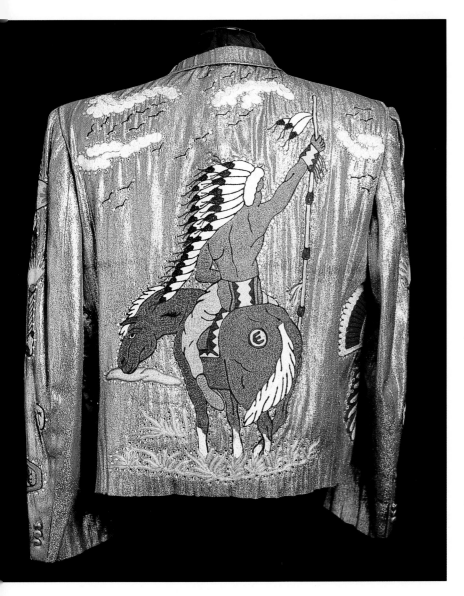

Nudie pulled out all the stops for this Rex Allen suit jacket, made about 1960. (Country Music Hall of Fame collection)

*F*rontex suit (left),
reminiscent of the
late 1930s, when
checkered billbilly
outfits were beginning
to combine embroidery
and western yokes
(William and Laura
Wynn collection).
California Ranchwear
suit (right) must have
been a winner; these
turn up all over the
country (Les and Teri
Berkowitz collection).
Both suits were made
between 1945 and
1955.

After the loud ties
faded, the tie bars
remained popular for
another ten years or
so. Tie bars, clips, and
clasps were popular
even through the
1960s. All the silver-
buckle companies
manufactured tie
accessories along with
money clips, cuff links,
watchbands, and
cigarette cases. Prices
ranged from a few
dollars for nickel
silver to several
hundred for diamond-
eyed longhorns set in
silver and gold. (High
Noon collection)

Western wear in black-and-white was rarely seen until the late
1950s. Leather hat by Tony Lama, embroidered trousers, and
sterling bolo with branded tips (Tyler and Teresa Beard
collection); embroidered Frontier shirt. (Les and Teri Berkowitz
collection).

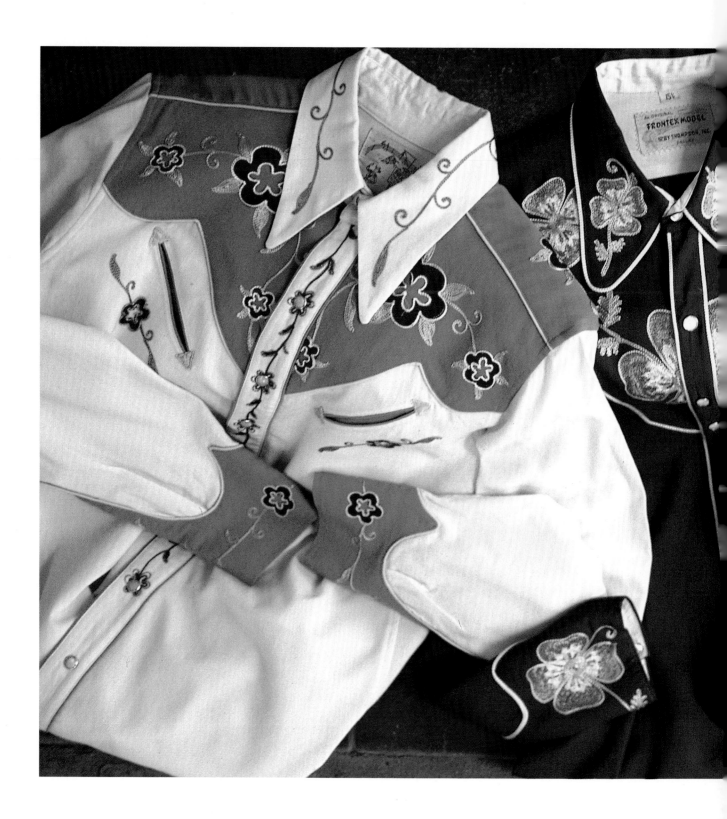

*T*hree doggone good suits made by (from left to right) Buck Bernie, The Cowboy Tailor, Los Angeles; California Ranchwear; Irby Thompson. Killer shirts like these vary in value from $300 to $600. (High Noon collection)

In the 1940s and 1950s, many women's blouses had buttons rather than western snaps, for a broader public appeal. The various makers shown here are H Bar C (for Porter's), The Corral, and Connie Sportswear. All of these were made in Denver, Colorado, which has always been the hotbed of western-wear manufacturing. (High Noon collection)

*Y*ou wouldn't mind someone turning their back on you if they were sporting one of these western doozies. In the back is a Sunflower shirt by Sam A. Formann (Les and Teri Berkowitz collection). The shirt on the left is by Frontex, which sold at Oshmans Sportswear in Houston, Texas. On the right is a magnificent example of a Rodeo Ben. (Left and right from William and Laura Wynn collection)

NORFOLK PUBLIC LIBRARY
NORFOLK, NEBRASKA

WESTERN TIES

Western air-brushed, hand-painted, and hand-decorated ties started up in the late 1930s and remained popular through the 1950s. Till Goodan, a well-known cowboy artist in the '30s and '40s, had his designs on numerous ties which have now become very collectible. His daughter, Betty Goodan Andrews, in 1992, began reproducing a line of ties with her father's original designs. Vintage ties can fetch anywhere from $35 to $200.

*R*alph Lauren was the first designer to revive the serape coat, vest, and skirt in 1988, but this blazer was styled by Rodeo Ben of Philadelphia about 1950, which proves that classic clothing designs never die; they just go to high-fashion heaven. (National Cowboy Hall of Fame collection)

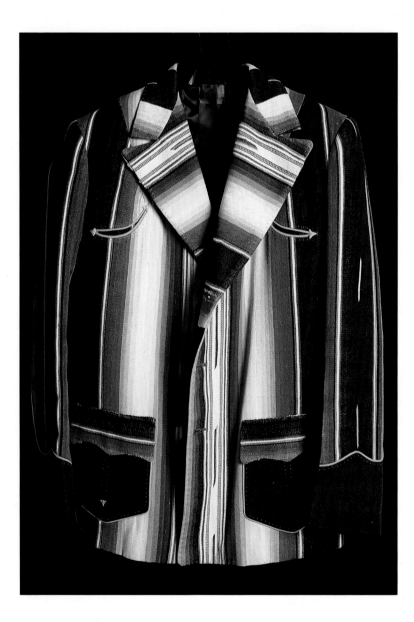

*T*his caboodle is owned by Linda Kohn. (High Noon collection)

It would have been hard to beat this off-the-rack Western Ranch Wear of California shirt in the 1950s. (Les and Teri Berkowitz collection)

A basic black boot with engraved sterling toe tips and heel guards, maker unknown. Toe tips and heel caps were worn as early as the 1920s but never achieved great popularity. They have become faddish with the rock-'n'-roll and punk-cowboy movement. (National Cowboy Hall of Fame collection)

These Justin boots were a gift from Buck Rutherford to June Ivory, both famous rodeo celebrities in the 1950s. Fashioned from purple calfskin, the vamps and uppers are inlaid with padded roses and gold leaf designs. (National Cowboy Hall of Fame collection)

*S*ome little buck could find in this catawampus collection exactly what he needed for a day's adventure on the urban prairie in the 1950s. (Gary van der Meer collection)

*T*he yellow and hot pink-trimmed wool gabardine shirt is by Sam A. Formann of Buffalo, New York. Very little is known about Sam, but all of his clothing is recognizable by the exaggerated geometric scooped yokes and the silk-cord top trim which outlined the collars and cuffs (Tom Bailey collection). The shirt on the right is a tasty, highly stylized western-motif shirt by Frontier (William and Laura Wynn collection).

*T*he McClure family in Fort Worth, Texas, made some fine western wear for the Fort Worth Fat Stock Show and Rodeo crowd in the 1950s. Their chain-stitch patterns resemble N. Turk's style. (Tyler and Teresa Beard collection)

*A*ny cowboy or cowgirl worth their weight in
*r*hinestones wouldn't be caught onstage without
a pair of boots like these. (Mark Hooper collection)

Judy Lynn, "Miss Show Business," reportedly spent over a half million dollars on her wardrobe with Nudie before she retired in 1980. Judy appeared in rodeos as halftime entertainment, riding her white horse, who was decked out in tack and saddle that matched her outfits. She would sing a little, do a few horse tricks, then ride out of the arena in a spotlight burning the breeze and blinding the audience with her reflection. (Photo Country Music Hall of Fame)

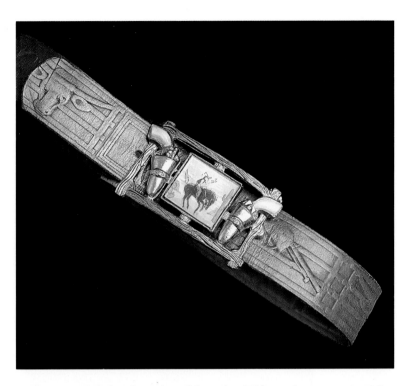

This Action Belt was the coolest of the cool in kiddie cowboy couture in 1962. (Tyler and Teresa Beard collection)

The finest pair of Nudie boots I've ever seen, made for Roy Rogers in the early 1960s. (Roy Rogers and Dale Evans Museum collection)

A deep purple wagon-wheel and cactus rhinestone suit has been Porter Wagoner's trademark since about 1960. Studded wide lapels indicate this suit was made in the 1970s. It's by Nudie. (Collection of the Grand Ole Opry Museum at Opryland USA)

PORTER WAGONER

Porter Wagoner was a recording star and Grand Ole Opry member when "The Porter Wagoner Show" started up in the early 1960s. His show was one of the top-rated country music shows in syndication all over the United States. A classic Porter Wagoner deluxe rhinestone suit can cost as much as $14,000. The boots are extra. Porter has remained true to his original style more than any other performer in country music. Porter, we love it. Don't ever forsake your rhinestone roots.

Lefty Frizzell and Gail Davis (Annie Oakley of the TV series) showing off their rhinestones and fringe by Nudie. (Photo Country Music Hall of Fame)

The narrow lapels indicate this Porter Wagoner suit was made by Nudie in the early 1960s. (Photo Country Music Hall of Fame)

1970–1990

THE FALL OF WESTERN WEAR:
HIPPIES, POLYESTER, WESTERN GRUNGE,
URBAN COWBOYS AND REDNECK CHIC

By the mid-'70s, the poor old cowboy didn't know what hit him. *Western Horseman* magazine, the cowboy bible, began to run some pretty scary ads, with cowboys not quite lookin' like cowboys and cowgirls lookin' more like daughter Judy of the Jetsons. I call this period the "dark ages" of western wear. The tailors and manufacturers continued to provide high-quality workmanship, but the styles and fabrics took an aesthetic nosedive. Catalog and magazine ads were showing ultra-suede pant suits, bell bottoms, checkered jeans and flared slacks, medallions, knee-high lace-up moccasins, Billy Jack hats, western leisure suits made from 100-percent polyester and Kodel, patent-leather boots with antique finishes and patchwork tops, and hats with macrame hatbands and decorated with feathers. Everything during this period was guaranteed not to wrinkle, fade, or breathe.

Just when we thought it couldn't get any worse, in the late '70s, Willie Nelson's grunge look began to take hold. Willie and his Nashville outlaws promoted a style that can best

Western wear had struck an all-time low here—rock bottom. Mid-1970s his-and-her matching 100-percent polyester western leisure suits by Panhandle Slim were called Pace Setters. (Photo courtesy Panhandle Slim)

be described as "red-neck hippy." Then in 1980, just about the time everybody had their embroidered and rhinestoned denim jackets coordinated with Charlie 1 Horse hats, John Travolta's *Urban Cowboy* was released. The western floodgates opened and the "red-neck chic" era was born.

It's fascinating to remember that at this time, leisure suits and Nudie suits were both in vogue. Massive round-toed clodhoppers and cockroach killers were equally acceptable. The same year (1980), Sandra Kauffman's *Cowboy Catalog Book*, an instructional and entertaining guide, led fledgling cowboys and cowgirls through the what's-hip-and-what's-not maze of western wear.

Although the '70s cast a giant shadow over the '80s, the cattle were getting restless. *Silverado* was the stepping off point in 1985, for the revival of the 1890s Old West style. This was the beginning of public interest in authentic cowboy gear and collectibles; vintage western wear was getting a second chance. As it turned out, the 1980s were a proving ground and clearing house for the '90s.

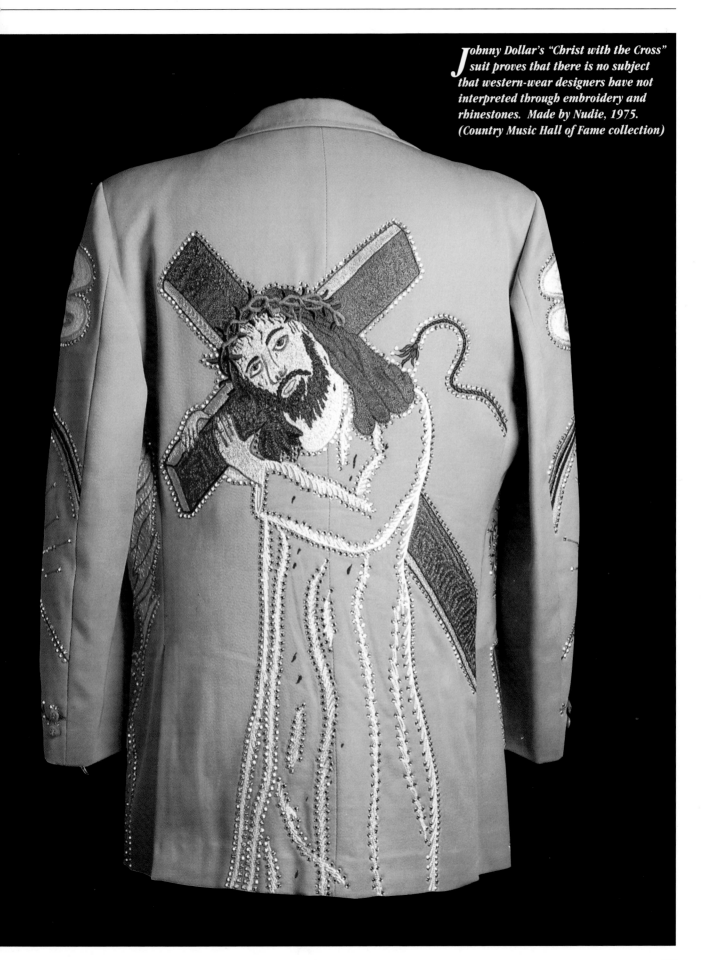

Johnny Dollar's "Christ with the Cross" suit proves that there is no subject that western-wear designers have not interpreted through embroidery and rhinestones. Made by Nudie, 1975. (Country Music Hall of Fame collection)

I just can't picture petite Fern Sawyer holding up the weight of this twenty-pound three-piece pink rhinestone suit during a performance. Made by N. Turk, 1970s. (National Cowgirl Hall of Fame collection)

When he was
as a small ch
I can stand b

It took some
self-conscio

"At first, I use
and not even
recalled in la
were all laugh

Starting on te
"really scare

"All week lon
sleep, thinkin

However, Mar
shyness. And
behind the de

Marty's chara
reaching out
others to him
enthusiastica
because they
heart.

Brocades, satins, lamé, and stretch lurex were the fabrics preferred by cowgirls in the 1960s and early 1970s. Without the need of embroidery machines and rhinestone-setting devices, flashy garments were easily made in these fabrics at home or by local seamstresses. This jacket was "Made by Edna" and worn by Rhonda Sedgwick Stearns, 1965–75. Billie Hinson McBride wore the gold metallic leather boots with rhinestones made made in 1965–75. (National Cowgirl Hall of Fame collection)

Manuel made Marty Robbins a series of this exact outfit in a variety of colors—hot pink, purple, electric blue, black, white, and canary yellow. Every one of them was exactly the same. The belt, the hat, and the flying-nun lapels popular in the mid-1970s, bell bottoms, and cloth-covered boots were all embroidered with silk flowers and birds. (Collection of The Grand Ole Opry Museum at Opryland USA)

Nudie in the 1970s with his best customer, Roy Rogers. (Photo Country Music Hall of Fame)

The Unsinkable Freckles Brown, famous rodeo cowboy of the 1940s and '50s, posed for photographer Irving Penn in this Wrangler magazine ad from 1973. It's hard to believe, but the checkered polyester flared leisure pant was what Wrangler was pushing at the time. (Photo courtesy Wrangler Jeans)

115

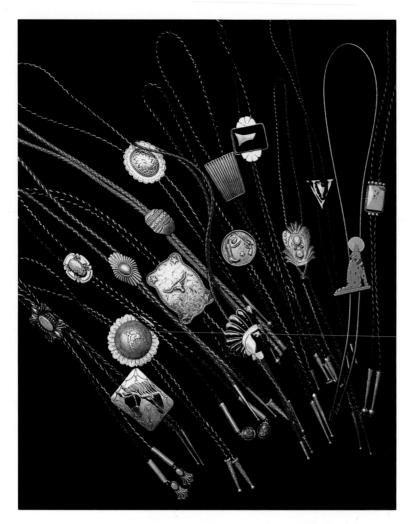

1890–1990
GALLERY OF WESTERN WEAR

In 1946 Jack Weil, founder and owner of Rockmount Western Wear in Denver, received a gift from a silversmith buddy in Wickenburg, Arizona—a small bar of silver folded over and engraved with slots for a boot-lace tie to fit through and be worn around the neck. Jack, who always recognized a good idea, called his friend, and they began to manufacture the first bolo ties, named after the South American tool used by cowboys to rope cattle. Bolos are a western-wear standard and come in an array of shapes, sizes, and materials. Today Rockmount alone offers more than two hundred varieties of bolos. (Jim Arndt collection)

When Lonesome Dove came out, it was critically acclaimed all over the world. We were in need of a historically correct western epic. The film influenced clothing manufacturers to begin making collarless bib-front shirts. Suspender sales skyrocketed and the custom boot shops were deluged with orders for tall-top boots. Mail-order Old West outfitter companies were swamped with sales, especially of the old gold-rush-style canvas ducking vests and pants. "Gus" hats were seen everywhere and have now become a standard request at hat shops, along with old and new favorites such as "RCA," "Texas Peak," "Dogger," "Roper," "Association," "Cattleman," "Horseshoe," "Four Corners," "Hoss," "Ruff 'n' Tuff," "Booger," and "George Strait." (Photo courtesy Robert Duvall Productions)

*D*enim: worldwide, in all languages, the word means the same thing—blue jeans. Levi Strauss patented his riveted pants in 1873. While there have been dozens of denim companies, the big three—Levi, Lee, and Wrangler—have dominated the market. In Japan, collecting and wearing vintage denim is practically a national pastime for the young. Big E, silver buttons, red line, buckle back, and pleated front are the collector's catchwords spoken with reverence by denim aficionados worldwide. (Tyler and Teresa Beard collection)

A variety of old belts, ranger sets, and trophy-style buckles. The buckle designs—in gold, silver, and turquoise—have been limited only by the makers' imaginations. (Tyler and Teresa Beard collection)

*T*his chain-stitch embroidered Indian head and feather pictorial shirt designed by Nathan Turk for a man was sold in a gift shop at Yellowstone National Park in the 1940s. Trousers with feathers and arrows running down the outside of the legs were also available. (William and Laura Wynn collection)

*O*ne-of-a-kind Manuel
jacket in black wool
gabardine with near-solid
silk embroidery and
rhinestones is not
recommended for the shy.
Batteries not included or
needed.

*E*questrian Lynn Randall
wore this red Don Hoy
hat with rhinestone trim
and hatband. Red satin
blouse was made by Maude
McMorries with fancy
yokes and pearl snaps. The
rhinestone belt by M. L.
Leddy and Sons, San
Angelo, Texas, has sterling
silver and gold overlay.
The boots are made from
Geoffrey's cat skin (South
America) by Nocona Boot
Company, Nocona, Texas.
(Photo courtesy Cowboy
Hall of Fame)

*G*ene Autry, legendary western clothes horse, owned literally hundreds of suits like this one by Nudie's of Hollywood. Everything Gene owned, even his guitar, was custom made. Belts, buckles, boots, and hats, along with all of Gene's clothing, were made by a variety of talented craftsmen. (Photo courtesy Cowboy Hall of Fame)

*F*etching boots from the
1940s and 1950s. The
yellow boot belonged to
rodeo cowboy Nay Cherry; its
heel and toe caps are
sterling silver with gold
initials. (Boots from the
collections of Tyler Beard,
Mark Hooper, and Gary van
der Meer)

*I*n the 1930s, some little buckaroo was a dude in cream-colored calfskin chaps with red calf trim, "ride
'em cowboy" kerchief, bench-made red boots with white and yellow inlay design, and spotted leather
wrist cuffs. His older brother, who was not quite into being a buckaroo, merely sported his bench-made
black boots with simple red stars and an oversized hat. Twenty some-odd years later, he bought his son
the little black horseshoe jacket, and the western-wear tradition in one family goes on and on and on . . .
(Tyler and Teresa Beard collection; horseshoe jacket Gary van der Meer collection)

*S*o you want to dress like a real old-time
1890s cowboy? This is what you need:
stovepipe boots with a high heel, California-
style spurs with silver coin conchas, leather
vest with pockets for cigarette "makin's," a
pocket watch, a wide-brim tall-crown Stetson
hat, hand-tooled wrist cuffs, spaghetti-fringe
shotgun chaps, holster and cartridge belt.
This 1874 pistol has carved Mexican eagle
grips, and the extra spurs would have been a
luxury item. Your canteen, slicker, blanket
and saddle bags with a few days' rations are
tied to your saddle and you're ready to hit the
trail. (Joe Gish Collection)

The induction into the wonderful world of western wear begins early out West. (Photo by Jim Arndt, courtesy Wrangler Jeans)

Western wear has always borrowed from and blended with the Indian arts. The blouse in plum color rayon with machine embroidery and a candy-stripe piped edge is new from ABS Company. The 1954 garment bag is hand-tooled and was won by Harry Tomkins, all-round cowboy and world-champion bareback rider. Collar tips are sterling with gold boots and garnets, made by Diablo, 1950–60. Beaded vest is vintage 1920–40 with floral designs and a deerskin back, which replaced its original calico-lined silk backing. (Tyler and Teresa Beard collection; collar tips William and Laura Wynn collection)

A 1989 Ralph Lauren suit in wool with trade blanket and serape designs trimmed in leather. The blouse is a two-tone rayon snap style with western yokes. The leather-laced hat is also Polo Ralph Lauren. (Laura Wynn and Teresa Beard collections)

Dudette duds, 1940s style. Fringed buckskin split-leg riding skirt, manila elkskin vest with elkhorn buttons. Frontex embroidered blouse with chain stitch, cotton cowboy motif neckerchief, topped off by a hair-on calfskin bow tie. The well-worn fringed riding gloves with red felt stars obviously served some cowgirl well. Wild West cowgirl silk-embroidered fringed gauntlets (1880–1920) somehow survived in pristine condition. (Tyler and Teresa Beard collection)

Yo, Tyler, can we take some of your hats and real West Texas cowboy boots out on the porch to shoot?" said Jim. "Yo," said Tyler.

The 1990s
WESTERN COUTURE GOES WILD:
100 YEARS OF INFLUENCE COME TOGETHER

In order to analyze what has happened to western clothing in the final decade of the century, you first have to divide the population into segments: rodeo folks, working cowboys and cowgirls, and urban wish-I-weres.

The rodeo cowboys and cowgirls of the '90s have uniforms—a rigid dress code in and out of the arena. This western style is innocently androgynous. These folks model themselves after mainstream country music stars: George Strait, Clint Black, Garth Brooks, and Brooks and Dunn. Women in rodeo must maintain this style on their own, because lately, all of the women in country music are wearing dresses, leather, and rhinestoned and embroidered Manuel jackets on the Grand Ole Opry and TNN. This rodeo crowd prefers the original roper boots or Justin Lace-up Ropers. None of these followers of fashion would be caught dead in anything but Wranglers. (This style of jeans became popular in 1974, when Wrangler became the official sponsor of the Professional Rodeo Cowboy Association. Before then, the Lee Cowboy Cut and Levi 501 were preferred by rodeo performers from the 1940s through the 1960s.) Painted Desert, Roper, and Mo Betta (popularized by Garth Brooks) are the shirts of choice. Brooks and Dunn also have endorsed a new line of shirts by Panhandle Slim. All of these draw heavily from the designs of the 1960s. Two-toned mods, psychedelic, and paisley

Yep, looks like a cowboy's work gear in the 1920s. But look again, some of the items are old and some are brand new. (Tyler and Teresa Beard collection)

125

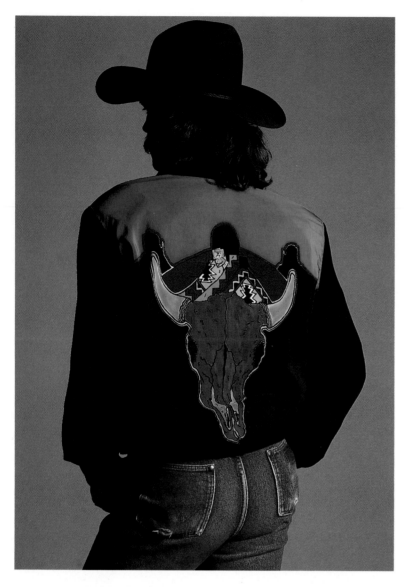

This Riflefire jacket is hand-painted by Amado Peña. Shoot, it must be good if Roy Rogers, Clint Black, Holly Dunn, The Bellamys, Steven Warner, and Paul Overstreet wear it. Riflefire is located in Nashville and specializes in hand-painted leather and silk clothing for men and women. (Jim Arndt collection)

patterns and glow-in-the-dark colors are not really new. Rodeo cowboys were wearing bright, free-flowing print shirts of rayon and satin in the late 1920s and '30s. Even the Bat Man-style cape across shirt backs today were worn in the 1960s; check out Steve McQueen in *Nevada Smith* (1966). Rockmount Ranch Wear has its finger on the pulse of the '90s, with remakes of some of their classics from the '40s and '50s, including cowboy-motif ties, '50s-style denim jackets, embroidered shirts, 100-percent cotton twill snap-up shirts, and bib-front and two-toned shirts in rayon with whipcord, top-stitching, and diamond-shaped pearl snaps. The hat is always basic black with a

manufactured George Strait crease.

The working cowhand is a different breed altogether. As in the past, most prefer to maintain some individualism in their appearance. Get any number of working cowboys together and you will see a variation in spurs, boots, hats, and gear, along with facial hair reminiscent of the 1890s ranch hands. You might see a well-worn hat with a lone star poked in the side of the felt with a toothpick for ventilation. You'll see tall crowns and short crowns, low brims and high. Boots can be anything from short to tall, as long as they have plain bottoms and bright-colored tops. Their spurs might have moons, arrows, stars, or even "The Alamo" or a girlfriend's initials in silver on the side. Don't be fooled: these men and women are keenly aware of their role in perpetuating ranching traditions of the West.

The tone of the urban wish-I-were movement is "anything goes": red-neck, mountain man, Santa Fe, rhinestone, working, rodeo, Old West, and "Young Rider" styles all work in the '90s. We now have the freedom to indulge our western fantasies at any level our bank accounts can afford.

In the '90s we have seen a revival of the peewee boot of the 1940s, and all of the boot factories are including remakes of golden-age boot styles in their lineup. The Calamity Jane and mountain man revival of deerskin or elkskin leather vests, jackets, skirts, pants, and anything you can hang fringe or beads on, has become mainstream western wear. Even our pajamas, boxer shorts, and socks are printed with cowboys and cowgirls on broncs or roping steers.

Everybody keeps asking, "When is this western craze going to end?" Trends do come and go, but in the 1990s we have seen a cowboy craze unlike any before. Perhaps the further we move away from our past, the

more desperately we try to capture the essence of it. City-slicker dude-ranch vacations are now all the rage, booking up a year in advance—something we have not seen since the 1950s. Western wear again has sex appeal, due in part to the strong and rugged individuals who typify the cowboy myth. The romantic appeal of the ranch lifestyle is evidenced by a mass exodus from golden California to Montana and Wyoming—the last frontier.

Looking back on a century of western wear, one thing is clear to me: the more things change, the more they stay the same.

A copy of a mid-nineteenth-century jacket with Indian and military influences. To create the twisted fringe, it was soaked in water and twisted until dry. (Jim Arndt collection)

In the '90s, deer and elkskin vests, pants, skirts, jackets, gloves, beaded belts, and gauntlets are refined throwbacks to the hippy movement of the 1960s and '70s. (Clothing courtesy of Billy Martins Western Wear)

*T*rophy-style buckles
in the last ten
years have adapted
not only classic
cowboy and Indian
designs, but
contemporary
silversmiths have
expanded the visual
range way beyond
"All-Round Cowboy
1972." (Jim Arndt
collection)

*T*his vintage
western shirt looks
as good with jeans,
boots, and a turquoise
western belt in 1990
as it did back in 1950.
(Tyler and Teresa
Beard collection)

A common sight out West these days—a 1990s rodeo cowboy in *a psychedelic button-up shirt, black hat, laced belt with trophy buckle, Wrangler 13MWZ jeans, wide-toed boots with a not-too-high heel and short-shanked rodeo spurs. (Photo by Jim Arndt, courtesy Wrangler Jeans)*

JAIME CASTANEDA

Jaime Castaneda began his tailoring career at Nudie's in 1974. In 1976 he left to pursue a 17-year position as head tailor with Manuel. When Nashville lured Manuel away from Hollywood, Jaime chose to remain behind. Now working alone from his home, with the help of his wife and embroidery magician Rose Clements, Jaime continues to follow in the rhinestone footsteps of his mentor, Manuel. Jaime is rapidly building a clientele of Nashville and Hollywood celebrities, sharing the responsibility of keeping Dwight Yoakam and other stars in their flashy duds. Remember the branded, rhinestoned, fringed shirt (copied from a Roy Rogers classic) on the 1993 Grammy Awards? That was Jaime. He also created Dwight's deerskin-fringed, lace-up shirt with matching pants for his CD *This Time*. Keep your golden needle threaded, Jaime.

"G*imme . . . gimme . . . gimme a redneck girl." From high fashion runways of New York City to the dusty ranch roads of the West, well-worn denim and broke-in leather are American favorites. This look is being reinterpreted by Ralph Lauren's RRL label, a line of motorcycle-cowboy clothing, à la Harley-Davidson meets John Wayne. (Redneck: Jill Momaday; clothing courtesy Back at the Ranch, Santa Fe, NM)*

*D*wight Yoakam moved to Los Angeles in the mid-1980s to play in the cow-punk honky-tonks of Hollywood. Dwight is a country traditionalist who put the hillbilly back in country music in a way that made it palatable for young country-music fans. Dwight has five albums and a number-one hit, "The Streets of Bakersfield," a duet with his mentor Buck Owens, to his credit. Buck who always wore Nudie suits, was also the inspiration for Dwight's rhinestone image. Here, Dwight is wearing his standard "RCA" felt hat. The jacket is white with silver metallic applique and layered rhinestones. The "I can't sit down" leather pants have laced bottoms and silver conchas. The rough-out boots are by Paul Bond; the clothing is by Manuel. (Photo courtesy Dwight Yoakam)

*W*endy Lane's Back at the Ranch in Santa Fe
is the only store in the country that sells
only used and vintage western wear—boots,
chaps, spurs, shirts, belts, buckles, and an array
of denim, along with used working-cowboy hats
complete with real live sweat, dirt and dust,
and flamboyantly decorated cowboy and cowgirl
hats by Hondo Hats.

Managers at Billy Martins Western Wear, New York City, sitting one out at the downstairs boot bar (from left): Collette Neyrey-Morgan, Gary van der Meer, Elizabeth Fowler, and Carroll Watts. Billy Martins has been the premier western-wear clothier to locals, celebrities, and tourists since 1978. (Photo © 1993 by Robert Essel, courtesy Billy Martins Western Wear)

At Jane Smith women's western-wear store, Jane (in the buckaroo boots) Kit, Nathalie, Debra, Jill, and Ana will help cowgirls' and wannabe cowgirls' dreams come true. Click your boot heels together three times and say, "I wanna go to Santa Fe, I wanna go to Santa Fe . . ." The store design by L. D. Burke and furniture by Burke and Sweet Water Ranch add a touch of western whimsy and romance.

Folks, one phrase comes to mind—Cowboy Class with a capital C. We will never see the likes of these cowboys again. At age 86, Gene Autry looks great and is still going strong. We caught up with Gene and his wife, Jackie, at the Autry Hotel in Palm Springs, California. "Trails of Happiness, Gene."

Roy Rogers, "King of the Cowboys," is fit as a fiddle at age 81. "Happy Trails, Roy."

*J*an Faulkner designs leather, suede, fringed, rhinestoned, and studded clothing for women and men. Left: black suede jacket with gold leather piping, and longhorns and lariats laid out in brass and bronze studs. Center: butterscotch-colored leather jacket with red leather piping, arrow pockets, and star inlays over the shoulders, with sterling buttons and an array of spots. Right: it takes thousands of metal spots to create this intricate cactus, horseshoe, longhorn, lariat, and star jacket. (Clothing by Jan Faulkner, courtesy Texas and Company)

Manuel Cuevas was born in Coalcoman, Mexico, about 1933. His older brother Adolfo taught Manuel to sew two pieces of cloth together at age seven. By age twelve, Manuel was working in a tailor shop. "In my area of Mexico, all men, women, even children were wearing white cotton clothing with a big red waist sash. I decided to make myself a peacock blue jacket, so I guess it was always there," said Manuel. As a child, he would walk four or five miles to the picture show to escape in the adventures of the Lone Ranger, his hero. He soon realized his dream was to come to America, where "I could create garments in the great American tradition but make them mine, make them more flamboyant."

In the mid-1950s, Manuel moved to Los Angeles. He worked briefly with N. Turk and Viola Grae, who taught him how to embroider. His longest stint as a young tailor was with Sy Devore, a Hollywood tailor. About 1960 Manuel took a job at Nudie's, sewing shirts. Nudie soon realized that Manuel was a volcano of creative designs waiting to erupt. Nudie immediately named Manuel his new shop foreman. "Nudie treated me like a king, he told me to try new things, I suddenly had the freedom I had been dreaming of."

Manuel married Nudie's daughter, Barbara. Their marriage lasted eleven years; the marriage to Nudie lasted fourteen. From 1960 to 1974, Manuel worked at Nudie's as the driving force behind trend-setting fashion innovations. Nudie then spent most of his time greeting customers and promoting his business, and being Nudie—that was a full-time job.

In 1974 family tensions caused Manuel to leave Nudie's and open his own shop down the street. Although there were hard feelings, there was plenty of glitz and glitter to go around. Freddie Hart gave Manuel $10,000 cash to help out with the move, and Mel Tillis came by the first week and ordered $70,000 worth of clothes for himself and his band. Manuel's following included Marlon Brando, Salvador Dali, John Lennon, Hank Williams, Jr., Glen Campbell, ZZ Top, Janis Joplin, Mick Jagger and Keith Richards, Bob Dylan, Neal Young, The Osmonds, The Eagles, Burt Reynolds, Johnny Cash, and the list goes on and on. "While at Nudie's or my own shop," said Manuel, "during my years in California, I made clothing for every star you can think of."

It is legendary that Manuel's clients place almost blind faith in his design ideas. "When I first met Elvis in the early 1970s, I asked him to show me a few stage moves. He began swaying his legs and I thought, 'What am I going to do?' Then I had the idea of a white rhinestone jumpsuit. Elvis told me to make it. When he saw it, he looked at it and said, 'What is this, overalls?' At the time, Elvis did not understand it, but he wore it and the rest is history."

Then there's the Linda Ronstadt story. "Linda Ronstadt and I go back a long way. I've made a lot of different clothes for her. Linda had just finished her first country album, *Trio*, with Dolly Parton and Emmylou Harris. She called and wanted me to make her a white dress. She said, 'I want it this way and that

way.' I said, 'No problem.' When she came to pick it up, she exclaimed, 'What is this?' I said, 'No white dress for you, kid. Put this on. It's what you really needed.' Linda wore the black dress to perform in that same night and loved it."

"Dwight Yoakam started it all in 1985," said Manuel, who remembers him playing in small clubs in Hollywood before he was discovered. "Dwight bought a hat in 1983 from me. He wanted it blocked in the 1960s 'RCA' crease ('Rodeo Cowboy Association')." Years later, in 1985, when Dwight finally got a recording contract, he headed for Manuel to redefine his image. What he wanted was a Buck Owens bolero jacket dripping in rhinestones. After Dwight's second album, *Hillbilly Deluxe*, came out, the record company received more than three thousand letters and calls wanting to know where they could get a jacket like Dwight's. Now half of Nashville's musicians are wearing the bolero style, and most western-wear manufacturers have short-waisted jackets in their clothing lines. That one jacket is what got the rhinestones rolling again.

In 1989, at age 58, Manuel closed his shop in Los Angeles and moved his entire business to Nashville. Now located in a beautifully restored Victorian house, Manuel seems very content and happy to be in Nashville. His demanding clientele still draws him out to Los Angeles every so often for measurements. One of his two daughters, Morelia, age twenty-four, has moved from Los Angeles to Nashville to learn her father's business. Norma Paz and seven other full-time employees handle the workload for Manuel, clothier to the Nashville music scene.

Among the younger country music stars who have beaten a path to Manuel's door are Wynonna Judd, The Desert Rose Band, Highway 101, Alan Jackson, Sawyer Brown, David Allan Coe, Mark Chestnutt, Travis Tritt, and Michelle Wright. In recognition of his highly successful career designing for celebrities and the television and movie industry, Manuel was the recipient of the prestigious MODA award in 1992.

Manuel talks more like a renaissance man than anyone I have ever met. His favorite color is the sun, and his favorite color combination is black and gold. When he speaks of American fashion influence on himself, he means literally all the Americas—the continent. Drawing upon his Mexican heritage, Manuel designed, in traditional style, all of Linda Ronstadt's clothes for her "charro girl" look for the "Canciones de Mi Padre Tour." He will discuss for hours how buttons are made, various craftsmen, boot makers, fabrics. Anything beautiful, Manuel appreciates it. "Native American Indian designs and their heritage have always fascinated me. That is why I have always used Chimayo blankets and silver and turquoise buttons.

"Since 1960 Manuel has been an integral part of western wear, with Nudie and without. Manuel continues to wave his magic western wand over all who meet him. Thanks to Manuel and Dwight Yoakam, the golden age of western wear is in full swing once again. Thank you, Manuel, western wear's renaissance man.

*M*anuel, legendary tailor to the stars, in his shop in Nashville.

*R*ed gabardine waist jacket with floral silver and gold metallic thread embroidery, accented by rhinestones and Indian-inspired concha buttons. Made by Manuel.

*C*ream gabardine jacket covered in western figural embroidery with "Frankenstein" laced arrows, which began to appear on clothing in the late 1930s. Manuel still uses classic rhinestone buttons and delicate topstitching prevalent on western clothing since the 1950s.

*M*ost of the western jewelry in the '90s imitates the kitschy style of the '40s and '50s. *(Jewelry courtesy of Billy Martins Western Wear, Jane Smith, and Nathalie Kent)*

*S*ilver concha belts and turquoise have always gone hand-in-hand with western wear. The trend these days—
with women and men—is to layer two or three belts at a time. (Belts courtesy Billy Martins Western Wear
and Back at the Ranch)

*R*anger buckle sets consist of a buckle, a tip, and one or two keepers. The big guys in the buckle business are Sunset
Trails, Vogt, Boblin (all of them), Doug Magnus, Zora Joe, RDM Company, Scottsdale, AK, Jeff Deegan, Chacon, and
James Reid. (Belts, buckles, and badge courtesy Billy Martins Western Wear)

The Maverick western-wear store is located in the historic stockyard area of Fort Worth, Texas. The Maverick carries a complete line of mid-range and high-end western wear for men, women, and children. Inside the store is an old-time saloon bar, where cowboys and cowgirls can sidle up to Japanese and French tourists taking a break from the rigors of shopping with a refreshing sarsaparilla or Lone Star beer. At the bar Steve Murrin, Gale Hill, and Angie Cumbie take a break.

At Hondo's Hats, Rusty Cox and Becky Patterson's specialty is old and new western hats, aged or decorated with cutouts of stars, moons, cactus, and other western designs. They add horse-hair hatbands, stampede strings, conchas, bone and antler buttons, cowhide, rawhide, lacing, and beadwork. No two hats are alike. In addition, Becky and Rusty customize fringed gauntlets, vests, jackets, and denim with applique, silver, and fabric mosaics. There ain't nothin' these two can't do.

*T*he new trend in western-wear stores is far removed from the warehouses of the '70s and '80s, with stacks of hats, jeans, boots, and mile-long racks of look-alike shirts. Out of Santa Fe is a perfect example of the new breed. Thoughtful western interiors utilize cowboy and Indian arts and antiques for decoration and display. Specialty designers, local artisans, and small manufacturers who specialize in the "golden age of western wear" revival styles are prominent in the '90s marketplace. (Photo courtesy Out of Santa Fe)

Contemporary western "Ranger" buckle sets on a variety of hand-tooled and exotic belts. All of these buckle sets are sterling silver and 14K gold, with genuine sapphires and rubies. (Buckles and belts courtesy Two Moons)

***W**orking cowboy and poet Ross Knox knows he was born a hundred years too late.*

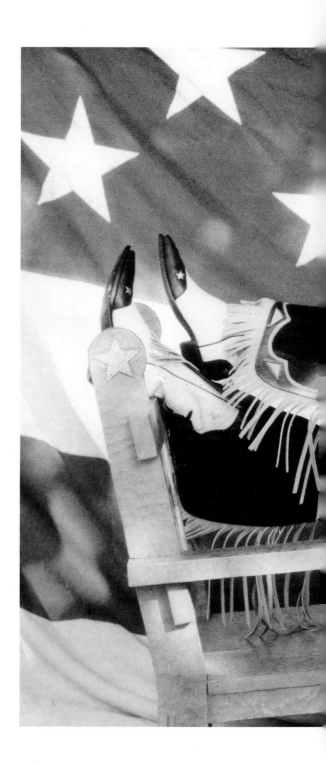

*H*igh-fashion rodeo gear is popular with big and little
cowgirls. Woman's shirt by Chad Cox, child's shirt
is vintage, chaps by Barstow Show Chaps, hat by Tom
Hirt. (Photo by Tony Kent; model Jackie Volker, courtesy
Elite/L.A.; child model Tara Kent; clothing and furniture
courtesy Jane Smith)

*H*igh-fashion rodeo gear that's never yet seen the inside of a
rodeo arena. Charro coat by Riders of the Century, chaps
by Barstow Show Chaps. (Photo by Tony Kent; model Jackie
Volker, courtesy of Elite/L.A.; clothing and furniture courtesy
Jane Smith, Santa Fe, NM)

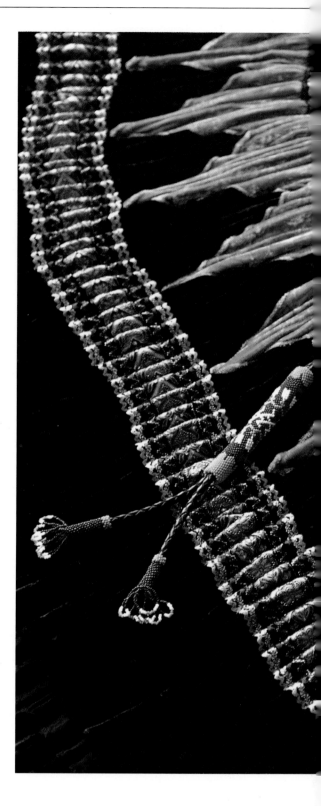

***P**orter Wagoner, 1990s style. He never gave up his rhinestoned threads. Suit by Manuel. (Photo courtesy Porter Wagoner)*

*B*lack velvet broomstick-pleated skirt reminiscent of square-dance clothing, with turquoise velvet and metallic rickrack. The matching black hat has a beaded hatband, brim roll, and decorative stampede string. (Clothing courtesy Billy Martins Western Wear)

Santa Fe locals Jack Pressler and Spencer Kimball turn heads everywhere they go, dressed in clothing from their vintage collections.

Kathy Smith, clothing designer and costumer for Dances with Wolves *and* Son of the Morning Star, *blends cowboy, Indian, and military style to create high-fashion clothing. (Cowgirl Nathalie Kent; jacket courtesy Simply Santa Fe; other clothing, jewelry, and boots courtesy Jane Smith)*

*T*he demand for vintage western textiles to satisfy the coat and vest market has been so great that most fabric companies now have a cowboy line for clothing and upholstery. Top: coat made from 1960s cowboy bed blanket; left: cowboy coat made from a 1950s bedspread with sterling concha buttons; right: a 1950s Roy Rogers bedspread made into a coat; bottom: vest made from contemporary cowboy fabric. (All clothing courtesy Bank at the Ranch)

Cowgirl, 1990s style. Jacket by Manuel. (Photo courtesy Tony Kent and Jane Smith, Santa Fe, NM)

SOURCE GUIDE TO RETAIL STORES AND CUSTOM WESTERN TAILORING

There are thousands of western-wear stores nationwide. Consult the Yellow Pages for the store nearest you. Check under western wear, boots, hats, cowboy, ranch stores, feed stores, and saddle shops. You will find western clothing sold in a variety of places.

To find out when and where you can see custom leather goods, horsehair, beadwork, jewelry, belts, buckles, spurs, and everything else in the world that a cowboy or cowgirl would wear, subscribe to *Rope Burns,* Box 35, Gene Autry, OK 73436. This magazine covers all activities of interest to the western-wear fan and collector.

ARIZONA

Cattle Company Cowboy Exchange
Rucker Rd., Milepost 12
P.O. Box 27
Elfrida, AZ 85601
(602) 824-3540
New western wear.

Corral Western Wear
5870 E. Broadway
Tucson, AZ 85711
(602) 747-2117
New western wear.

Laradas Western Store
756 W. Main St.
Mesa, AZ 85201
(602) 834-9339
New western wear.

Saba's (10 locations in AZ)
18 W. Main St.
Mesa, AZ 85201
(602) 833-0753 for the store nearest you
New western wear.

Stockman's Western Wear
4648 N. 16th St.
Phoenix, AZ 85016
(602) 279-5814
New western wear.

CALIFORNIA

Jaime Castaneda
11443 DeLano St.
North Hollywood, CA 91606
(818) 766-8781
Custom western tailoring.

Duckhorns Tack and Western Wear
18154 Hwy. 18
Apple Valley, CA 92307
(619) 242-3002
New western wear.

Falconhead
11911 San Vicente Blvd.
Los Angeles, CA 90049
(310) 471-7075
New western wear.

Howard and Phil's
    (53 locations in AZ, CA, NV, UT)
19415 Soledad Canyon Rd.
Canyon Country, CA 91351
(805) 252-8931 for store nearest you
New western wear.

Jacob Roberts Ltd.
2843 S. Hill St.
Los Angeles, CA 90007
(800) 421-9083
Reproduction western ties with original artwork by Till Goodan, famous western artist of the '30s and '40s.

Jonathan's
1705 S. Catalina Ave.
Redondo Beach, CA 90277
(310) 373-8708
New western wear.

Harvey Krantz
4247 Freedom Dr., Suite 507
Calabasas, CA 91302
(818) 222-4326
Custom western tailoring.

Nudie's of Hollywood
5015 Lankershim
North Hollywood, CA 91601
(213) 877-9505
Custom western tailoring.

The Old Frontier Clothing Company
P.O. Box 691836
Los Angeles, CA 90069

221 N. Robertson Blvd., #D
Beverly Hills, CA 90211
(310) 264-9378
Reproduction Old West clothing.

Out of Santa Fe
297 Newport Center Dr.
Newport Beach, CA 92660
(714) 644-5953
New western wear.

Red River Frontier Outfitters
P.O. Box 241, Dept. CD
Tujunga, CA 91043
Reproduction of Old West clothing.

Thieves Market (14 locations in CA)
(714) 380-7700 for the store nearest you
New western wear.

Western Corral
7734 Girard Ave.
La Jolla, CA 92037
(619) 551-9595
New western wear.

Box T Hat Company
Tom Hirt
P.O. Box 560
Penrose, CO 81240
Custom hats.

Cry Baby Ranch
1422 Larimer Square
Denver, CO 80202
(303) 623-3979
Vintage western wear.

Greeley Hat Works
549 N. 71st Ave.
Greeley, CO 80634
(303) 353-7300
New western wear.

Texas and Company
601 E. Hopkins
Aspen, CO 81611
(303) 925-8323
Cowgirl couturier.

J. W. Cooper
3015 Grand Ave., #177
Coconut Grove, FL 33133
(305) 441-1380

7494B N. Kendall Dr.
Dadeland Mall
Miami, FL 23156
(305) 663-6235

3015 Grand Ave., #175
Coconut Grove, FL 33133
(305) 447-1627

9700 Collins Ave., Rm. 147
Bal Harbour, FL 33154
(305) 861-4180
New and vintage western wear.

GEORGIA

Geronimo's
3234 A Roswell Rd. Atlanta, GA 30305
(404) 233-3234
New and vintage western wear.

IDAHO

Ross Western Wear
207 E. Main
Jerome, ID 83338
(208) 324-4500
New western wear.

ILLINOIS

Out of the West
2187 N. Clybourn Ave.
Chicago, IL 60614
(312) 404-9378
New western wear.

Wunderlich West
704 N. Wells St.
Chicago, IL 60610
(312) 943-2354
New and vintage western wear.

INDIANA

Tonto Rim Trading Company
Box 463
Salem, IN 47167
(800) 242-4287
Hats.

IOWA

River Junction Trading Company
312 Main St.
McGregor, IA 52157
(319) 873-2387
Reproduction Old West clothing.

KANSAS

Sheplers Western Wear
(19 stores in AZ, CO, KS, MO, NV, OK, TX)
(800) 835-4004 (for free catalog or the
store nearest you
New western wear.

LOUISIANA

J & H Boots and Jeans
5218 Cypress
West Monroe, LA 71291
(318) 396-2407
New western wear.

MASSACHUSETTS

T. P. Saddleblanket Company
152 Main St.
Great Barrington, MA 01230
(413) 528-6500
New and vintage western wear.

MINNESOTA

Schatzlein Saddle Shop, Inc.
413 West Lake St.
Minneapolis, MN 55408
(612) 825-2459
New western wear.

MONTANA

Miles City Saddlery
808 Main St.
Miles City, MT 59301
(406) 232-2512
New western wear.

Rand's
2205 1st Ave. N.
Billings, MT 59101
(800) 346-9815
Custom hats.

David Viers
Park and G Streets
P.O. Box 1374
Livingston, MT 59047
(406) 222-7722
Historically correct construction of pre-1920s boots.

NEVADA

J. M. Capriola Company
500 Commercial St.
Elko, NV 89801
(702) 738-5816
New and reproduction western wear.

D Bar J Hat Company
3873 Spring Mountain Rd.
Las Vegas, NV 89102
(702) 362-4287
(800) 654-1137
Custom hats.

Sam's Town Western Emporium
P.O. Box 12001
511 Boulder Hwy.
Las Vegas, NV 89121
(702) 454-8017
New western wear.

Tip's Western Wear and Custom Saddles
185 Melarkey St.
Winnemucca, NV 89445
(702) 623-3300
New western wear.

NEW MEXICO

Back at the Ranch
235 Don Gaspar
Santa Fe, NM 87501
(505) 989-8110
Head-to-toe vintage western wear.

P. T. Crow
114 Amherst S.E.
Albuquerque, NM 87106
(505) 256-1763
New and vintage western wear.

Mark Hooper
721 Quincy S.E.
Albuquqeruqe, NM 87108
(505) 256-0321
Vintage western wear.

Jack Pressler
920 Don Juan
Santa Fe, NM 87501
(505) 983-3547
Vintage western wear.

Jane Smith
122 W. San Francisco St.
Santa Fe, NM 87501
(505) 988-4775
Top-notch cowgirl couturier.

Monte Cristo Hat Company
118 Galisteo
Santa Fe, NM 87501
(505) 983-9598
Custom hats.

The Rainbow Man
107 E. Palace Ave.
Santa Fe, NM 87501
(505) 982-8706
Vintage western wear.

Rancho
322 McKenzie St.
Santa Fe, NM 87501
(505) 986-1688
Vintage and serious outdoor clothing by Schaefer Outfitters and Filson.

James Reid
114 E. Palace Ave.
Santa Fe, NM 87501
(505) 988-1147
Belts, buckles, and accessories.

Simply Santa Fe
72 E. San Francisco St.
Santa Fe, NM 87501
(505) 988-3100
Fine women's western wear.

NEW YORK

Billy Martin's Western Classics
812 Madison Ave.
New York, NY 10021
(212) 861-3100
(800) 888-8915 for a catalog
The finest new western wear in the Northeast.

Katy K Designs
79 Washington Pl., #3R
New York City, NY 10011-9136
(212) 254-2975
Custom retro western wear.

H. Kauffman's and Sons
419 Park Ave. S.
New York, NY 10010
(212) 684-6060
(800) 872-6687
Western and equestrian wear.

Polo Ralph Lauren (27 stores in the U.S.)
867 Madison Ave.
New York, NY 10021
(212) 318-7000 for the store nearest you
Fine western and equestrian wear.

Whiskey Dust
526 Hudson St.
New York, NY 10014
(212) 691-5576
New and vintage western wear.

OKLAHOMA

Cowboy Classics
Box 333
917 N. Main
Fairview, OK 73737
(405) 227-4307
Western luggage, purses, and accessories.

Wells Western Wear
6251 New Sapultapasa Rd.
Tulsa, OK 74131
(918) 446-3363
New western wear.

OREGON

D. W. Frommer II, Bootmaker
308 N. 6th
Redmond, OR 97756
(503) 923-3808
Historically correct construction of old cowboy boot styles and packers.

TENNESSEE

Manuel
1992 Broadway
Nashville, TN 37203
(615) 321-5444
Custom western tailoring.

Riflefire
1801 21st Ave. S.
Nashville, TN 37203
(615) 297-6241
The Riflefire line and other contemporary western-wear designers.

TEXAS

Antēks
5812 W. Lovers Ln.
Dallas, TX 75225
(214) 528-5567
Western T-shirts and accessories.

Blue's Western Wear
100 Main St.
Gustine, TX 76455
(915) 667-7215
New western wear.

Boot Town (6 retail stores in TX)
(214) 243-1151 for the store nearest you
New western wear.

Cavalry Regimental Supply
Box 64394, Dept. H
Lubbock, TX 79464
No phone
Reproduction Civil War and Indian War cavalry boots.

Cavender's Boot City (6 stores in TX)
(817) 589-2180 for the store nearest you
New western wear.

Copper Star Trading Company
Box 10066
Amarillo, TX 79116-1066
(800) 828-0442
Cowhide clothing and accessories.

Cowboy Trappings
2739 N. Main St.
Fort Worth, TX 76106
(817) 626-3882
New western wear.

Frontier Western Wear
205 N. Mason
Bowie, TX 76230
(817) 872-3572
New western wear.

Harry's Western Wear
  (also in San Saba, TX)
126 W. Central
Comanche, TX 76442
(915) 356-3151
New western wear.

Hondo's Hats
101 E. Austin,
Fredericksburg, TX 78624
(210) 997-8007
Custom hats and clothing.

Joe's Western Wear
113 N. College St.
Waxahacie, TX 75165
(214) 938-9378
New western wear.

Just Justin (2 retail stores in TX)
1505 Wycliff
Dallas, TX 75207
(214) 630-2858
New western wear.

JZ Ranchwear
1537 K Ave.
Plano, TX 75074
(214) 422-9980
New western wear.

Lone Star Boot (2 stores in TX)
(214) 445-0277 for the store nearest you
New western wear.

The Maverick
100 E. Exchange St.
Fort Worth, TX 76106
(817) 626-1129
New western wear.

The Prairie Schooner
Main St.
Buda, TX 78610
(512) 295-3448
Vintage western wear.

River City Tattoo
513 E. 6th St.
Austin, TX 78701
(512) 476-8282
*See Diamond Glenn for the type of western
wear you can't take off.*

Sargeant's Western World (2 stores in TX,
     1 store in IL)
13600 Stemmons Fwy.
Dallas, TX 75234
(214) 247-0855 for the store nearest you
New western wear.

True West
P.O. Box 48
Comanche, TX 76442
(915) 356-2140
*Men's, women's, and children's vintage
western wear.*

Two Moons Trading Company
3411 Rosedale
Dallas, TX 75205
(214) 373-8822
Buckles, belts, and accessories.

Western Warehouse (2 stores in TX)
10838 N. Central Expressway
Dallas, TX 75231
(214) 891-0888
New western wear.

Wild Bill's
West End Market
Dallas, TX 75202
(214) 954-1050
New western wear.

Woodard Western Wear
412 N. Center St.
Bonham, TX 75410
New western wear.

U T A H

Hey Charlie
P.O. Box 4587
541 Main St.
Park City, UT 84060
(801) 647-7767
New western wear.

V E R M O N T

T. P. Saddleblanket
Rts. 11 and 30
Manchester Center, VT 05255
(802) 362-9888
New and vintage western wear.

W A S H I N G T O N

Jan Faulkner
914 24th Ave., S.
Seattle, WA 98144
(205) 329-5874
Custom western tailoring.

Ruby Montana
603 2nd Ave.
Seattle, WA 98104
(206) 621-7669
Vintage western wear.

Simon's Tack and Tog
9210 S. Tacoma Way
Tacoma, WA 98499
(206) 588-4546
New western wear.

WYOMING

Cattle Kate
3530 S. Park Dr.
Jackson, WY 83001
(307) 733-7414
New western wear.

Cheyenne Outfitters
380 N. American Rd.
Box 29
Cheyenne, WY 82003
(307) 775-7500
New western wear.

Creations in Leather
1031 12th St.
Cody, WY 82414
(307) 587-6461
(800) 457-7560
Custom leather clothing.

Custom Cowboy Shop
321 Main
Sheridan, WY 82801
(307) 672-7733
New western wear and custom leather.

King Saddlery
184 N. Main St.
Sheridan, WY 82801
(307) 672-2702
New western wear and custom leather.

Lov Inc / Jackson Trading
P.O. Box 36586
25 W. Broadway
Jackson, WY 83001
(307) 733-2114
New and vintage western wear.

Lou Taubert Ranch Outfitters
125 E. 2nd Ave.
Casper, WY 82601
(307) 234-2500
New western wear.

Weather Hat Company
1384 Coffeen Ave.
Sheridan, WY 82801
(307) 674-6675
Custom hats.

Wild Turkey
Box 601
35 W. Deloney
Jackson, WY 83001
(307) 733-4719
New western wear.

Museums Where You Can See Vintage Western Wear

There are dozens of museums of coast to coast with collections of Old West clothing. Check the museum nearest you. You might be surprised: even the Smithsonian in Washington, D.C., has a fine collection.

ARIZONA

Rex Allen Museum
150 N. Railroad Ave.
Willcox, AZ 85643
(602) 384-4583

CALIFORNIA

Gene Autry Western Heritage Museum
4700 Western Heritage Way
Los Angeles, CA 90027-1462
(213) 667-2000

William S. Hart Museum
24151 San Fernando Rd.
Newhall, CA 91321
(805) 254-4584

Roy Rogers and Dale Evans Museum
15650 Seneca Rd.
Victorville, CA 92392
(619) 243-4547

OKLAHOMA

Tom Mix Museum
721 N. Delaware
Dewey, OK 74029
(918) 534-1555

National Cowboy Hall of Fame Museum
1700 NE 63rd St.
Oklahoma City, OK 73111
(405) 478-2250

TENNESSEE
Country Music Hall of Fame
4 Music Square East
Nashville, TN 37203
(615) 256-1639

Opryland USA Museum
2802 Opryland Dr.
Nashville, TN 37214
(615) 871-5987

When in Nashville, be sure to visit all the privately owned museums listed on the maps to the stars' homes. They all have great clothing.

TEXAS

Joe Gish Old West Museum
502 N. Milam
Fredericksburg, TX 78624
(512) 997-2794 (By appointment only)

National Cowgirl Hall of Fame Museum
P.O. Box 1742
515 Ave. B
Hereford, TX 7945
(806) 364-5252

Panhandle-Plains Historical Museum
2401 4th Ave.
Canyon, TX 79016
(806) 656-2244

Texas Rangers Hall of Fame
I-35
P.O. Box 2470
Waco, TX 76702-2570
(817) 750-5986

WYOMING

Buffalo Bill Historical Center Museum
Box 1000
Cody, WY 82414
(307) 587-4771